W9-BMK-690

Reagan's America

REAGAN'S AMERICA

LLOYD DEMAUSE

CREATIVE ROOTS, INC., PUBLISHERS

Box 401, Planetarium Sta.   3 Henrietta Street
New York, N.Y. 10024   London, WC2E 8LU
U.S.A.   England

REAGAN'S AMERICA

LC82-73581   ISBN 0-940508-02-8

DeMause, Lloyd.
    Reagan's America.

Includes bibliographical references and index.
1. United States — Politics and government — 1981-
2. United States — Foreign relations — 1981-
3. Reagan, Ronald — Personality. I. Title.
E876.D45   1984   973.927   82-73581
ISBN 0-940508-02-8

For Neil and Jennifer

Author's Foreword

This book is the story of the feelings and the fantasies that we shared in Reagan's America.

My main goal has been to show why it is that in politics—as in our personal lives—the conditions which we deplore are so often those which we unconsciously desire, often bringing upon ourselves some of our most painful historical events.

An understanding of why this should be so requires some patience on the part of the reader. Because the book is the result of the analysis of thousands of documents, a certain amount of evidence must be presented before the reader can see the shared fantasies hidden in the evidence. I ask from the reader only to be patient enough to allow this evidence to begin to accumulate in the chapters that follow. Before long, the patterns will make sense, even when they contradict common opinion as to our motives during the Reagan years.

For it is not difficult to describe what happened in Reagan's America. It is only difficult to believe that we wanted it that way.

Lloyd deMause
New York City
April, 1984

Contents

1

THE SHOOTING OF RONALD REAGAN
"The King Must Die"

From the very beginning, something seemed to be out of control in Reagan's America.

If ever there was a time in history when America should have felt strong and happy, it was at the beginning of the 1980s.

We were not at war. The Iranian hostages had just been returned home safely. There was no domestic violence or major strikes at home. Both economically and militarily, we were the strongest nation on earth, with the highest Gross National Product, the least number of people living in poverty and the highest personal income at any time in our history.

What is more, America had created 20 million new jobs in the past decade and had made major advances in providing for basic nutritional and medical needs for its poorest families, all without any increase in government repression, without major domestic strife and without war.

We had every reason to be proud of what we had accomplished in the 70s and to look forward to the tasks of the 80s secure in the knowledge of our ability to achieve further economic and social progress.

For some reason, however, our success in the previous decade made us feel just terrible. Never before in history had a nation so strong and wealthy felt so weak and impoverished. Ronald Reagan was elected president in what could only be described as an atmosphere of crisis, with the media everywhere filled with predictions of dangers of economic collapse. As he assumed office, our new president voiced what we all felt:

we were not strong at all, but "weak and disintegrating." He said he felt like a captain of a "ship about to go over the falls," and that we were "in

When Jimmy Carter became president, cartoonists showed him as a savior who could walk on water.

When Ronald Reagan became president, cartoonists showed him as taking over a sinking ship.

greater danger today than we were the day after Pearl Harbor." We were, in fact, so weak, he said, that we were in danger of being totally impotent before "an evil force that would extinguish the light we've been tending for 6,000 years."

The main reason why we felt we were "about to go over the falls" was said to be our "precarious economic condition." We were supposed to have failed particularly badly in three areas: a "soaring Federal debt," "low corporate investment" and "out of control inflation." Yet actual government figures showed these supposed "failures" were really more fantasy than reality. Federal debt as a percentage of Gross National Product was in fact not soaring but was the lowest in fifty years,[1] corporate investment was not low at all but was in fact the highest since World War II,[2] and even the twelve percent inflation rate at the end of 1980 was coming down fast in the early months of 1981, most of it having been caused by temporary conditions such as the jump in oil prices and higher food prices caused by bad weather.[3]

Yet our healthy economy and enormous military power had little influence on our shared fantasies of growing national impotence and imminent danger of disintegration. Polls showed how widespread our fears were: 75 percent of us believed that "the United States had gone off on the wrong track," 60 percent thought we might need a leader who would "bend the rules a bit," and 50 percent felt it might now be necessary to use force to restore "the American Way of Life."[4] Drastic measures of all sorts were seriously discussed by politicians for the first time in decades as ways to restore our depleted strength. The result was the election of Ronald Reagan as president, with his radical new "Program for Economic Recovery" and with plans for over a trillion dollars in additional military spending designed to restore our national potency.

The imagery used by the media—imagery which so often reflects our shared feelings—embodied our shared fantasies of impotence and growing anger. Contrary to the normal presidential pattern of an initial "honeymoon period" when the imagery reflects feelings of strength and hopefulness,[5] Ronald Reagan was seen as totally beleaguered by dangerous beasts which he was barely able to hold off with slashing

The beasts of the world seemed under our control during Carter's first year.

The beasts of the world seemed out of control as Reagan took over.

sword strokes. Headline stories at the end of 1980 reported we felt ourselves to be "AMERICA, A NATION **BESET**. IT WAS A YEAR WHEN NATURE SEEMED TO REFLECT A **DARKENING** NATIONAL MOOD, WITH THE **EXPLOSION** OF **PENT-UP FURIES** AND A **PARCHING** OF THE SPIRIT AND THE LAND." (*N.Y. Times Magazine,* emphasis added.)[6]

Ronald Reagan's first speeches, too, reflected our "**darkening** national mood," our "**pent-up furies**" and "**parching** of the spirit." When he won the nomination, he told us that our country was "**disintegrating**," "**weakened**" and "**eaten away**." When he won the election, the most often used word in his acceptance speech was "**frightened**." In his Inaugural Address, he stressed such words as "**terror**" (of runaway living costs), "**doomed**" (what we need not be) and "**sacrifice**" (what we must now do). His first State of the Nation address consisted almost entirely of such apocalyptic language. If only the sentences which contained emotional terms are reproduced, his entire address reads as follows:

President's State of the Nation Address
February 5, 1981

We're in the worst economic **mess** since the Great Depression...the Federal budget is **out of control** and we face **runaway** deficits...inflation, **like radioactivity**, was cumulative and that once started it could get **out of control**...**Wars** are usually accompanied by inflation...we can lecture our children about extravagance until we **run out of voice and breath**...I've already placed a **freeze** on hiring...I've put a **freeze** on pending regulations...It will propose budget **cuts**...budget **cuts**...spending **cuts**...Prices have **exploded**...We will **unleash** the energy...we've let negative economic forces run **out of control**. We've **stalled** the **judgment day**...a **shattered** economy...

Reagan's choice of language was in complete contrast to the State of the Nation addresses of his predecessors. Rather than using the usual "honeymoon period" language reflecting feelings of strength and hope, he confirmed to us our own feelings that our country was "out of control...like radioactivity," and told us we would have to "cut...cut...cut" something or someone to prevent an apocalyptic "judgment day."

To take this one step further, if *just* the fantasy words (in **bold** type above) are considered, the essence of his address can be reduced to the following:

Fantasy Analysis of
President's State of the Nation Address
February 5, 1981

Fantasy Words	*Interpretation*
mess...out of control...runaway ...like radioactivity...out of control...wars...run out of voice and breath...freeze...freeze ...cuts...cuts...cuts...cuts exploded...unleash...out of control...stalled...judgment day...shattered	We feel like a mess, out of control, runaway, like radioactivity. We are so out of control that, as in a war, we are out of breath and freezing. We must cut someone or we'll explode and unleash our out-of-control rage, which, if not stalled now, will produce a final judgment day which will leave us shattered.

These feelings of disintegration and growing rage which we shared at the beginning of Reagan's presidency were not really rational feelings concerning objective economic conditions, as the president claimed. The State of Nation address above says that Federal expenditures, Federal debt and inflation were "out of control" at the beginning of 1981. A look at the actual figures for these three areas shows this to be quite untrue.

First the "runaway" Federal expenditures which we believed to be so out of control had, in fact, *shrunk* during Jimmy Carter's term as a proportion of Gross National Product,[7] mainly due to Carter's success in keeping military spending under control. (Percentage of GNP rather than absolute dollars is used as the most meaningful index for fiscal analysis, since only in this way can one see the proportion of one's earnings each year that is spent by the government.)

Secondly, the "out of control" Federal debt had in fact also *shrunk* in the past three decades to *one-half* the former percentage of GNP. What the Federal government owed was now only equal to 30 percent of a year's pay for each of us compared to 60 percent in 1950 and 110 percent in 1945. Rather than being out of control, Federal debt was actually only now becoming manageable. If we could only avoid huge deficits in the future it would shrink further to a rather insignificant portion of our annual earnings.

Thirdly, although the 12 percent average inflation rate at the end of 1980 was indeed higher than in many previous years, it was also true that two days prior to Reagan's State of the Nation address he had just been given the January 1981 inflation figures, which showed that inflation had just dropped to 9 percent. If in fact inflation as Reagan took over was going down—and if lower oil, food and interest costs were forecast by most economists to push the rate still lower in coming months no matter who was in office—then it was pure fantasy to say that inflation at that moment was "out of control like radioactivity."

Yet *something* seemed to be "out of control like radioactivity" in America. If it wasn't Federal spending, debt or inflation, then perhaps the feeling had something to do with *ourselves*. Perhaps it was *we* who for some reason seemed to feel "full of pent-up furies," perhaps it was *we ourselves* who felt "out of control."

Political commentators intuitively felt the power of this growing national feeling as they summarized the nation's mood at the beginning of Reagan's term. Flora Lewis reported in her *N.Y.Times* column that "Despite the relaxed banter of the President in news conferences...there is a low mean hiss to be heard in the land [as shown by] the snarling, deliberately nasty way people are coming to treat each other, with no immediate provocation but their own despair."[8]

Before Reagan was elected, he was seen as capable of wielding a knife.

The president himself picked up the angry mood in his language, as when he asked his budget-cutters to be "meaner than junkyard dogs," and in the media imagery of his early months. Rather than the usual "honeymoon" symbols of strength and confidence, the media showed our new leader surrounded by the brutal symbols of the ax, the knife, the hanging rope and the guillotine, accompanied by the murderous phrase "CUT, SLASH, CHOP" endlessly repeated until the emotional message could not possibly be missed.

Reagan's inaugural platform was felt to have been equipped with a guillotine.

"Reagan's ax" was everywhere in the headlines as he took office. Politicians, the media and the public all seemed entranced by the impending violence implied by the thousands of headlines and magazine covers boasting that "REAGAN READIES THE AX,"[9] or "THE AX FALLS"[10] or "REAGAN'S $50B AX! CUTS WILL AFFECT EVERY AMERICAN."[11] Although his "$50 billion cuts" were only in domestic programs, the fantasy was that he had drastically cut the budget.

Political commentators could barely restrain their delight at the coming effects of the sacrificial ax. "The president has brought a wonderful new mood to the federal bureaucracy—fear," said one journalist.[12] *Newsweek* promised us Reagan's term would be the "bloodiest in years."[13] Reagan himself announced that "the howls of pain will be heard from coast to coast" when what was called his "cut-slash-chop men began their cavalry attacks."[14] Polls showed the public supported his call for pain. As *Newsweek* put it: "POLLS: LET THE AX FALL."[15]

Hanging and cutting people were seen as Reagan's main tasks.

During the first few weeks of Reagan's presidency, the imagery of the bloody axing of people and their coming howls of pain seemed to be just what we needed to embody our growing rage. Only occasionally could we allow ourselves to feel our guilt about taking out our violent feelings on scapegoats. "Some of what Reagan is doing is great and some of what he's doing just scares me half to death," said one person interviewed, as he wondered how he felt about having voted for Reagan and about the prospect that "a year from now you're going to have people freezing and starving to death."[16] But more often our conscience was easily stilled with economic rationalizations. We usually could barely conceal our praise for what we were asking the Reagan team to do in our name. "I think you've been brilliant," Senator Metzenbaum told David Stockman at an early Senate Budget Committee hearing. "But I also think you've been cruel, inhumane and unfair."[17] We never questioned why anyone should be praised for being "brilliant" and "cruel" at the same time.

In the final analysis it was not David Stockman whom we admired for his "brilliant cruelty." It was Ronald Reagan. The same thing was true when we bestowed our praise on others in his administration for

The symbol of Reagan's presidency: the sacrificial ax.

their hardness. When columnist George Will praised Alexander Haig for having a "beautifully shining steel fist" in foreign policy, he was in fact also admiring *Reagan's* beautifully shining hardness. Only a leader that hard, only a president with a shining steel fist, could embody all the rage we asked him to contain for us.

The most important way we asked Reagan to embody our violence was by asking him to effect a military buildup three times as large as that of Vietnam.[18] Despite the fact that the world was unusually peaceful when Reagan took over, polls showed that Americans were nevertheless extremely belligerent in foreign policy at the beginning of 1981. *U.S.News & World Report* summed up the nation's feelings in a survey of opinion made in February of 1981 by citing New York City Mayor Ed Koch as saying "Reagan is reflecting the mood of this country. He is exhibiting the fact that the United States will not be pushed around."[19]

Reagan feeds the military as a container for our violent fantasies.

The mood behind the new military buildup was openly discussed by the press. "The fevers of war are once again upon us," reported *Harper's*. "They do not yet rage openly, but beneath the surface of recent American events can be felt the gathering strength of attitudes and emotions that permit us to think about war in ways that were impossible even a year ago. We hear almost daily the militant pronouncements of our political candidates and news of escalating appropriations for arms. We seem to be witnessing the remilitarization of America..."[20]

Other periodicals repeated the message, with varying degrees of fascination and alarm. The *N.Y.Times Magazine* featured an article on "RETHINKING THE UNTHINKABLE," with the second headline reading: "After more than a decade during which the idea was all but dismissed, the possibility of nuclear war is again on many people's minds. Some strategists believe it's an option that must not be ruled out—indeed, that such a war can be won. Others fear the entire world will lose." None of the articles tried to show that the new interest in winning a nuclear war was brought about by any real change in world conditions. Like the *Times*, they just noticed that inexplicably "nuclear war is again on many people's minds."

The New Republic captured the new mood perfectly in its article on "THE NEW BRINKSMANSHIP":

> For the first time since the 1950s, the possibility of nuclear war with the Soviet Union appears to be seriously accepted by key figures inside and outside the US government. What long have been unthinkable thoughts now are entertained by influential men and women in Washington....A senior White House foreign policy specialist says: "In 30 years, I never thought war was really possible: now I think it *is* possible..."[22]

It was left up to the women's section of the *N.Y. Times* to express directly our deepest feelings about "thinking the unthinkable" once again. Maggie Scarf, reviewing the literature on the "increasingly threatening reality" of engaging in atomic war, said simply: "I'm getting scared again."[23]

Ronald Reagan's own feelings about having to embody so much of our explosive anger were ambivalent. Most often, he indicated that as president he completely accepted his role as container for our poisonous rage. As *Time* reported in their first story on his presidency, at one early meeting "he fingered a jelly bean, and joked: 'They tell me the purple ones are poison,' then nonchalantly popped it into his mouth."[24] His language and actions usually showed him ready to act out our anger and resentment with enthusiasm. Only occasionally did he reveal some guilt and fear of being punished for carrying out his role. "I can assure you, by morning, I'll be hung in effigy," he forecast after an early budget meeting where he proposed slashing funds for the poor and disabled. His fears of punishment, of course, did not come about, since our reaction to his budget cutting was not to hang him in effigy but to praise him openly for his ability to "inflict pain...with nerve and verve."[25]

As Reagan's first month drew to a close, more and more media fantasy messages began to center on the question of whether he was in fact strong enough to be a container for our growing rage. It was as though we felt only a Superman, only a living Man of Steel, could really contain our explosive anger and act it out for us. Was Reagan really strong enough to be the "beautifully shining steel fist" we needed?

Earlier in history, after new kings were crowned, they, too, were often required to prove that they were strong enough to embody their people's violence. Often this was done by having the king engage in a ritual battle with a young warrior to prove his superior strength.[26] Similarly, at the beginning of his term of office, since Ronald Reagan was going to have to embody such an extraordinary amount of our anger, he would first have to undergo a trial of his strength if he were to be capable of being our leader in the coming years of "national renewal."

The fantasy that Reagan might die in office surfaced around the country even before his inauguration, in a series of "jokes" and published speculations, all of which revolved around his age and impending death in office. Most of them were based on the coincidence that no American president elected since 1840 in a year ending in zero had lived out his term of office. "Re-elect Bush in 1984" read one version which appeared on thousands of bumper stickers all over the country, and many other "death jokes" and articles about the "death jinx" multiplied during his first month in office.

The method of his trial was to be by shooting, not hanging, as Reagan himself implied in the phrase quoted earlier. Although death wishes toward a new leader are impossible to portray directly in the media, cartoons often pictured Reagan in conjunction with guns. Some, like the one below, even managed to show him standing next to several targets,

An early cartoon showed Reagan next to targets and guns.

with gun holes all around, and dozens of guns on the floor. Most often—as is usual when the media has to put forth unacceptable fantasy messages—the *content* of the message was stated openly, but the *object* was shifted away from Reagan. For instance, when Anthony Lewis labeled his *N. Y. Times* column at the beginning of 1981 "THE KING MUST DIE," he was overtly writing about Jimmy Carter.[27] Yet his startlingly direct headline, and his discussion of Mary Renault's novel about people who became kings and then are themselves killed, could certainly be taken as an unconcsious message that Reagan must die as well. Writing an article headlined "THE KING MUST DIE" just before a Presidential Inauguration could hardly be called a coincidence.

The climax for these shared fantasies that "the king must die" came in the final week of March. For no apparent reason, a growing number of articles had appeared during March discussing a "crime wave" which America was supposed to be undergoing at the time. As a climax to this flood of articles, both *Time* and *Newsweek* the week before the shooting ran almost identical covers and lead articles on the horrors of violent crime. (The coincidence is important, since both newsweeklies always keep their cover stories a secret from each other until the last moment, to prevent duplication of cover stories wherever possible.)

Time and *Newsweek* **ran identical cover stories the week before the shooting of Reagan.**

These lead stories, embodying our own growing violence, contained what must have been the highest percentage of violent imagery ever published in a lead newsweekly story. The fantasy words used in the articles contained virtually nothing but a long string of violent images, such as the opening of the *Time* article, which read "crime...murder...raped ...violence...crime...killing, robbing, raping and assaulting..." and so on, for page after page of extraordinarily frightening imagery, focused mainly on handguns.

That these scare stories on a wildly "out of control" crime wave were actually based on figures as fictitious as those of our supposedly "out of control" economy is more difficult to believe, so successful has the media been in recent years in claiming a dramatic increase in major crime in America. Yet the most careful studies, those by the National Council on Crime and Delinquency, actually show slight *decreases* in the incidence of and in arrests for major crimes in recent years, concluding that "criminal behavior remains roughly constant over the years, and that 'crime waves' are created by the human imagination."[28] Once again, the "out of control" feelings reflected our own fantasies, not reality.

Death in Washington shown the week before the shooting.

The covers of the other two major newsweeklies the week before the shooting likewise contained hidden assassination messages. *The New Republic* simply ran a cover which displayed gravestones in front of the Capitol Building and Washington Monument, a subliminal message of death wishes toward the head of government. *U.S. News & World Report*—whose editorial policy was more supportive of the president than *The New Republic*—was not as open about their death messages. Their cover pictured "Angry Americans" as "frustrated and losing ground" while an uncaring, rich father-figure stood above them as they dropped into a chasm. This alone, however, was not explicit enough to show what must be *done* by these "angry Americans" to the father-figure looking down upon them with so little sympathy. So the editors of the magazine put a

Waste—Reagan's Next Target

headline *above* the main headline which gave the fantasy message as a subliminal suggestion. The message, at first glance, seemed innocent enough. It read "$60 BILLION OF FEDERAL WASTE—REAGAN's NEXT TARGET." As is so often the case with deeply-denied fantasies, part of the headline actually contained two hidden messages:

Waste—Reagan's Next Target
Waste Reagan
(Kill Reagan)

Reagan's Next Target
(Reagan Is the Next Target)

In addition to these assassination messages appearing on the front covers and lead stories of our national newsweeklies, headlines and pictures in many of the daily newspapers in the few days before the shooting showed an upsurge in violent language, death imagery and gunshot victims.[29] So unprecedented was the number of hidden messages to shoot the president, that at a meeting of The Institute for Psychohistory, where hundreds of periodicals and newspapers were being analyzed for their fantasy content during the week before the shooting, concern was voiced about the possibility of some disturbed individual picking up such a flood of hidden suggestions and acting upon them.[30]

One other person picked up the assassination messages at the same time as the gunman did: Alexander Haig. For no apparent reason, during the week before the shooting Haig suddenly began a big fight with others in the Reagan administration about "who will be in charge in case of emergencies" if the president should be incapacitated. At one point, two days before the shooting, Haig even argued about his primary role in the cabinet "in line of succession" to the presidency, as though "succession" were for some reason about to become an issue. The succession discussion merged so closely with the actual events on the day of the shooting that Haig's statement seemed to merge in the memory of most people with his proclamation just *after* the shooting that "As of now, I am in control." The reason, of course, why so far no one has questioned why Alexander Haig began talking about "succession" just before the shooting was that in a real sense the same unconscious assassination wishes he was acting upon were shared by the entire country.

One more person, of course, picked up the assassination messages displayed on tens of millions of magazine covers and newspapers that final week in March: the gunman, John W. Hinckley, Jr. Needless to say, there are at all times many potentially violent people wandering around America with guns in their pockets and murder in their hearts, fantasying killing the president as a representative in their confused minds of figures of authority from their family life. But generally they wait for permission from others—in fact, for a *delegation from others*—before actually trying to commit the act, as did Oswald when he waited until he read similar subliminal assassination messages in Dallas newspapers before shooting John F. Kennedy. (The subliminal messages were so powerful that President Kennedy even unconsciously picked them up two months before his assassination and made a home movie "just for fun" showing himself being assassinated.)[31] Hinckley had been stalking both President Carter and President-elect Reagan with guns in his possession for the previous six months, but just couldn't "get himself into the right frame of mind to actually carry out the act," as he later put it. It was not until March 30th, he said, when he got what he termed "a signal" from a newspaper[32] and told himself "This is it, this is for me," that he walked out and shot Reagan.

Americans were, of course, genuinely upset to learn that someone had actually carried out their fantasies of assassination, but on a deeper level they were relieved too. To begin with, there were the numerous newspaper reports about school children who cheered when told that the president had been shot. Beginning in Texas, and later spreading to Oklahoma, Missouri and Minnesota, newspaper articles appeared which read like the following:

THE 7TH GRADERS WHO CHEERED THE NEWS
THAT THE PREZ WAS SHOT

A group of 7th graders cheered a school announcement of the attempt on President Reagan's life.

"I was dumbfounded. I didn't know what to do," said John Zannini, a teacher at Tulsa Central Academy.

"Here were these kids cheering that the president had been shot. I didn't know what to say."

He said 10 of the 16 pupils in his English class cheered when the principal gave a report of the shooting over the intercom.

Zannini said he checked around and found that some students in the eighth grade had reacted the same way...."Three or four were laughing about it. They asked me if he (President Reagan) was dead. When I said no, that he was doing well, they snapped their fingers and said 'shucks.' "[33]

Other local newspapers describing similar cheering school children read much the same. Apparently the children had picked up the national mood just as their parents had, but were less successful in repressing their reactions.

Of course, most adults did not openly cheer when they heard the news of the shooting. Yet even they could admit, if asked directly, that some surprising feelings had gone through their minds when first hearing of the shooting. The only poll to actually ask people precisely what the first thought was which occurred to them after they had heard about the shooting found that about half admitted that their first thought was one of relief,[34] thinking "good" or "I laughed" or "I felt relieved" or "I wished he had had better aim" or some other identification with the shooting. The other half of those polled said the first thing that went through their minds was some form of conspiracy theory, such as "Haig did it" or "Bush did it" or "somebody wants to get revenge for the cuts he's made" or "the Russians did it." All responses, in other words, indicated that the shooting was equally *wished-for*, but the wish for the second half of those asked was attributed to some person other than the respondent. *No one* answered the poll by saying that they were surprised at the shooting.

The media reaction, too, was one of lack of surprise. Many articles recalled the earlier expectation that he would be killed in office. "PRESIDENT ONE INCH AWAY FROM BEING 8TH VICTIM OF ZERO YEAR JINX" was how the *N.Y.Post* reported the shooting, as though it was due to magical sorcery somehow in the air. Others simply admitted that the shooting was not unexpected, only the timing was off. Mary McGrory reported in her column that her immediate reaction on hearing that Reagan had been shot was the thought that "Reagan had been in office only 70 days. Yes, his policies alarmed and unnerved some. But he was a nice man, and nothing irretrievable had happened. It was TOO SOON."[35]

"Too soon," perhaps, but not unexpected, and somehow oddly a relief. The editorials during the week following the shooting seemed thoroughly puzzled by our feelings, by our lack of remorse, and particularly by the complete absence of any action on gun control. With James Gannon, editor of the *Des Moines Register*, the nation asked itself:

> ## WHY ISN'T REAGAN ANGRY?
> ## WHY AREN'T WE ALL ANGRY?

> A madman shooting the president wounds the entire nation grievously. Yet the reaction has been shock but not surprise. The question is merely: When will it happen again? Next month? Next year? Next president?[36]

The reason, of course, why we weren't either surprised or angry at the shooting was because so many of us unconsciously wanted it. The president had to be tested to see if he could really be tough enough to contain our anger. He had been, and he had come through with flying colors. He was indeed as hard as steel. He could be shot one inch from the heart and then spit out the bullets, all the while joking with the doctors. Nothing could stop him. "IRON MAN REAGAN" had shown himself as strong as steel, and could do anything we required of him. What's more just as ancient kings had gone through death-and-rebirth rituals at the beginning of their rule, so, too, Reagan had been put through a death-and-rebirth ritual, and had emerged stronger than ever. Our national rage *could* be contained in his "shining steel fist."

In the weeks following the shooting, all violent language in the media simply disappeared, and was replaced by images more appropriate to a new, strong president. Reagan's "honeymoon period" only then began, with stories not only about his own amazing *personal* strength but about how strong *the*

Reagan was seen as made of iron for surviving our test of his strength.

nation now felt. Most of these images were displaced to other strong, phallic objects, such as the space shuttle, which *Time's* cover story said "gives the U.S. a mighty life...shouts rose...high over the distant buttes...Powerful...delight...buoyant...exhilaration..." and so on.[37] A similar "mighty life" was given to Reagan's public opinion polls, which had previously slipped to only 59 percent approval before the shooting (as compared to 73 percent for Carter at the same moment), and *The New York Times* announced that Reagan now enjoyed a "SECOND HONEYMOON" with the Congress and the public.[38]

After the shooting, images of violence were replaced by those of strength.

Reagan's understandably shaky first speech to Congress after his shooting was experienced by the country and Congress in tones of pure hero-worship.

SPEECH BRINGS DOWN THE HOUSE

President Reagan took the roof off the Capitol last night as Republicans and Democrats cheered his triumphant return...."It was inspiring—absolutely inspiring," Sen. Alphonse D'Amato (R-N.Y.) told The Post. "President Reagan's speech was one of the most dramatic events I have ever witnessed in my 14 years in the Congress"..."It was thrilling...He out-Wayned John Wayne."[39]

"Iron Man Ron," John Wayne reincarnated, hardened in battle, could now be depended upon to be strong enough to embody our national rage and lead us, wielding his sacrificial ax, in the great task to come—the cleansing and renewal of our dying land.

Yet so far we have explained very little about the nature of the feelings with which we began Reagan's America. Where did all this anger come from in the first place? Why did Ronald Reagan start his presidency with such a buildup of feelings of impotence, disintegration and rage, feelings so powerful we needed an assassination attempt before we could experience the normal strength of the honeymoon period? If our economy and our crime rate weren't really "out of control" at the beginning of 1981, what was?

To answer these questions, we must return to the source of this buildup of rage and try to understand why we shared the fantasy that we were "slipping toward impotence" during the presidency of Jimmy Carter.

2

CREATING THE IRANIAN CRISIS
"Slipping Toward Impotence"

When Jimmy Carter became president in 1977, America was entering one of the most productive periods in its history. The Vietnam War, the Nixon impeachment effort and the Ford recession were safely behind us. Our major economic indicators were showing considerable strength. Real Gross National Product was growing at a vigorous 5 percent rate, inflation was still only at 6 percent and even the 7 percent unemployment caused by the Ford recession was on its way down.

Carter was initially pictured as a "strong" messiah.

Carter himself had been nominated during a convention which was overtly utopian in expectations. Reporters covering the convention described it as an "orgy of togetherness," saying it was "less a convention than a festival" and wondering how Carter and Mondale would be able to give "substance to their promise of a new millennium."[1] After he was elected president, Carter was pictured as a "born-again" messiah, someone who would lead America to a millennial rebirth...merely by his presence, with little effort on our part.

Since people only have such unrealistic wishes about their leader when they are actually feeling very depressed about themselves,[2] it is not surprising that

Carter's extreme messianic image soon began to decay. By September of his first year, his popularity in the polls began to decline and his media imagery changed from the "strong" imagery of his honeymoon period to those showing that his strength was "cracking." The occasion for this "cracking" of Carter's image was actually an insignificant event—Bert Lance's banking trouble—which was blown far out of proportion to its real importance in order to fit our new fantasy that Carter was growing impotent in solving our underlying depression. Whatever Bert Lance's banking troubles really were about, they had nothing to do with Jimmy Carter's running of the government. Yet, after the press magnified the importance of the affair, Carter was seen by columnists as a "political

Bert Lance was the excuse for the "cracking" of Carter's image, shown by a cracking egg.

incompetent" whose "shattered" image had left the presidency in a "dangerously weakened state."[3] Although it is a fact of American politics that all presidents decline in popularity during their first two

years, Carter's polls declined faster than most, and the language and imagery of the media were increasingly dominated by fears of his growing weakness.

In reality, our fantasies of Carter's growing impotence were directly in contrast to his actual success in running the government and managing a booming economy during his first two years. The more the economic indicators moved upward—a record four million people were added to civilian payrolls in 1977 alone—the more incompetent Carter was considered to be.

The same contrast was true of our evaluation of his running of foreign policy. The more successful Carter was

Carter was seen as increasingly impotent during his "cracking" phase.

in carrying out his pledge to engage in peaceful diplomacy—negotiating the Panama Canal Treaty, detente with Russia, a reduction in U.S. troops in Korea and the Camp David Mideast Peace Accords—the more he was accused of being an "ineffective leader abroad." *The New Republic* captured the attitude most succinctly:

WHEN IN DOUBT, DUMP ON CARTER

> It is hard to pick up a newspaper, foreign or domestic, without encountering the refrain EUROPEANS VIEW CARTER AS WEAK, UNSKILLED LEADER . . . "Our Most Ineffectual Postwar President" . . . Nowadays, there's no need to think about what to do. Just say, "Carter's ineffective" and everybody nods.[4]

Whatever the reason for our fantasies of growing impotence, the reality was quite clear: peace and prosperity seemed to have made us feel worse and worse about our nation's condition. At the very time when unemployment was at a five-year low, when inflation had been moderating and when production was expanding the fastest, a *Time* "State of the Nation" survey concluded that a majority of Americans felt "THE TROUBLE IS SERIOUS" in America. Between April 1978 and April 1979, *Time* reported, the number of people who thought that "the U.S. is in deep and serious trouble" jumped from 41 percent to 64 percent,[5] the highest despair rating in our history. It almost seemed as if peace and prosperity were the *causes* of our fantasies of "deep and serious trouble" and "presidential impotence."

Thoughtful reporters could not help but note this strange reversal of common sense, even when they found they couldn't explain why it might be so. *New York Times* reporter Bernard Gwertzman noted a "PARADOX IN FOREIGN POLICY. Carter Finds He Gets Less Support, Not More, When Relations With Soviet Union Are Smooth."[6] James Reston wondered why America seemed to focus so much on shortages, when in fact "it is our surpluses and not our shortages that are choking and strangling us."[7] Vermont Royster, writing in *The Wall Street Journal*, located the feeling of how growing prosperity can be accompanied by fears of something terrible about to happen:

> We've all had the experience one time or another. Everything's fine at home, the family's healthy, the children are doing well at school, the job prospers. Yet we awake in the night with an uneasy feeling that something bad is about to happen. Psychologists call it "free floating anxiety" . . . [8]

In fact, what psychologists actually call the "free floating anxiety" which people feel as a result of too much success is *guilt*, guilt about the success itself. And the "something bad which is about to happen" is actually the *wish* that something bad might happen to punish us for our growing success and pleasures.

It was as though in the middle of our prosperity during the Carter period a vindictive parental figure awoke in our collective heads, begrudging us our happy families and prosperous work. The more our lives became successful, the more a ghostly conscience disturbed us in the middle of the night to remind us that we should *not* enjoy more happiness than our parents had enjoyed during our childhoods. Statistics confirmed what our consciences felt: in 1978 we earned double the real income our parents had earned, on the average,[9] we had better health, more personal freedom, more sexual enjoyment, in fact, more of everything worth striving for . . . and it was making us feel terrible.

Just how bad national peace and prosperity made us feel can be seen by examining the fantasy words used in the president's news conferences during Carter's third, or "collapse" phase. Presidential news conferences are especially revealing, because reporters express the nation's feelings and shared fantasies in direct form, while the president answers by telling the nation what he intends to do to relieve our bad feelings. Here is a sample news conference from Carter's "collapse" phase. As above, only the strong emotional words and body images are considered.

Fantasy Analysis of
Presidential News Conference
March 8, 1978

Fantasy Words	*Interpretation*
Q: Deterioration? Collapse?	Q: Is our world undergoing deterioration? Will it collapse?
A: Deterioration...rapidly increasing...rapidly increasing...deterioration...deadlock	A: Deterioration is rapidly increasing. We feel deadlocked to stop it.
Q: Dead? Strains?	Q: Will we soon be dead from the strains?
A: Teeth...tensions	A: You feel like biting with your teeth to relieve your anger.
Q: Action? Action?	Q: Will you take action to help us?
A: Act...act immediately...tremendous pressure...crisis	A: I'll act immediately. I feel a tremendous pressure to relieve the crisis.

The fantasy that our increasing prosperity was producing a "tremendous pressure" which might lead to total collapse of our world reached its climax in 1979. Carter's Gallup Poll dropped from 67 percent to 39 percent approval in one year, the lowest presidential rating for that month since Truman. Newspapers regularly reported such opinions as "Carter is a weak president...Few in Washington dispute the President's weakness. His cabinet officers and his aides know it to be a fact. On Capitol Hill party friend and foe alike take account of it. The pollsters measure it; the press, for the most part, revels in it..."[10] *Newsweek* proclaimed Carter was now on "a downward crumbling path as America's decline accelerates." *The Washington Star* declared that America was

We poured our "collapse" fantasies into the Oval Office, and saw Carter as too weak to prevent our world from collapsing.

"SLIPPING TOWARD IMPOTENCE ACROSS THE GLOBE."[11] In one day, *The New York Times* carried two articles, the first telling Carter he must resign because he was "the weakest and most incompetent president since Martin Van Buren," and the second by a psychiatrist saying that Carter needed psychiatric treatment.[12] Speculations about Carter's sanity multiplied. One day when Carter simply delayed a speech he was about to give to the press, "the unexplained cancellation caused world-wide speculation that Carter had gone bonkers." His appointments secretary had to assure newsmen that "Carter was sane and in charge and knew what he was doing."[13] Mrs. Carter even had to be sent out to give several speeches in which she "went out of her way to defend her husband's mental...health."[14] Both Carter and the nation were fantasied to be "going crazy," so split were we between our actual peaceful exterior conditions and our "collapsed" interior state. Several magazines during the summer of 1979 ran front cover headlines reading "THE SUMMER MADNESS," and James Reston, in a column entitled "THE SUMMER MADNESS," wondered why "Washington was having a nervous breakdown" at that moment.[15]

That Jimmy Carter felt these crazy projections of ours acutely goes without saying. After all, the main function of a leader is to contain the feelings we inject into him and to *do* something about them. If we felt we were going crazy and disintegrating, *he* had to feel the same. If we felt we were dying, *he* must be made to feel *he* was dying.[16]

Suggestions that Carter should die proliferated during the summer of 1979. Carter was said to be "among the political 'walking dead,'" "buried politically" and "a terminal political case."[17] Cartoons increasingly showed him strangled, beaten to death or present at funerals. One major newspaper featured the following interview with a noted labor leader on their front page: "Is there any way the President can redeem himself in your eyes?" "Yes, there's one way he can do it." "What's that?" "Die."[18]

Now when people "go crazy" from too much success, one of the ways they often try to ward off

MIND SQUEEZE.

We felt like we were going crazy by the middle of 1979, as shown in this ad.

their mounting guilt and depression is by manic spending sprees. The most familiar example, perhaps, is the wild spending sprees of new

"IT'S FALLING! IT'S FALLING!"

Cartoonists saw Carter as falling and disintegrating.

celebrities. The underlying hope of this defense mechanism is that one can magically get rid of the guilt of having so much money by spending it foolishly.

Death images of Carter proliferated in 1979.

The same thing happens to large groups of people when they feel as if they have accumulated too much. Consumers begin spending more than they should, borrowing the difference. Businesses begin expanding more than they should, again with borrowed funds. Labor begins demanding excessive wages, oblivious of whether the costs can be absorbed. Corporations raise their prices faster than usual, regardless of the effect on sales volume. Banks begin lending more than is prudent, for increasingly risky ventures, both in the U.S. and abroad. Everyone seems to make more "mistakes" than usual. The result of all this manic activity is what is termed "an inflationary psychology." It is a shared manic fantasy, one that *follows* a period of prosperity and operates through the magical device of warding off the guilt and depression that go with prosperity through manic spending. As *Time* put it in an article on the causes of inflation:

> "People are to blame in part because they're greedy. They've got to have the bigger house, the extra car, the new refrigerator. And there's no waiting for a year or two, they've got to have it now." Officials agree...Chairman of the Council of Economic Advisers Charles Schultze blames 60% of the problem on the inflationary psychology that keeps spreading.[19]

Accordingly, the first result of the "collapse" fantasies after the steady prosperity of 1977-78 was a jump in inflation rates in 1979 from the 9 percent to the 14 percent range, as everyone began to participate in a manic attempt to spend more in order to get rid of their prosperity.

That this sudden jump in inflation was blamed on Carter's policies had a certain crazy logic . . . after all, wasn't it his successful running of our economy that had increased our guilt and made us feel so bad that we had to spend more to try to get rid of it and feel better? No one, of course, analyzed the sudden surge in inflation that bluntly. Usually, analysts were vague when blaming the inflation on Carter, preferring not to have to point out a particular policy of his that was responsible for it.

The "collapse" fantasies of the summer of 1979 dropped Carter's popularity polls below those of any previous president in American history, a condition I had predicted would occur two years earlier. In my book, *Jimmy Carter and American Fantasy*, and in a series of articles, speeches and radio broadcasts during 1977, I analyzed the patterns of shared fantasies of American presidents and forecast that by the summer of 1979 Carter's popularity would totally collapse. I further predicted that America would then call him impotent and ask him to find an "enemy" by the end of 1979 who would humiliate America and force us into a military confrontation.[20] Two years after these predictions, the national mood was precisely what I had said it would be. Hedrick Smith wrote a front-page article in *The New York Times* in June of 1979 calling American mood "politically explosive" and quoting a high administration official as saying "The American people are mad—hot-summer mad."[21]

Obviously something had to be done by the president, and soon. Carter retreated to Camp David for guidance. Like Moses, he went "to the mountaintop," listening to the voice of God: the people and their elected representatives. He jotted down in his diary some of the things the people told him while at Camp David:

> "Mr. President, we're in trouble. Talk to us about blood, sweat and tears."
> "Congress has collapsed . . . "
> "The people are just not ready to sacrifice."
> "There is a malaise of civilization."
> "Be bold, Mr. President."
> "If you lead, Mr. President, we will follow."[22]

Carter heard what the people wanted him to do. He had to be bold. He had to give them blood, sweat and tears. And he had to end their malaise by providing them with a sacrifice.

After Carter came down from the mountain, but before he had a chance to address the nation, several commentators speculated on what he would tell them must be done to cure the country's emotional crisis. Max Lerner told him how he must be a shaman:

CARTER'S MOUNTAINTOP POLITICS

The leader today must be a practitioner of magic, a tribal shaman who calls on the unseen spirits to work their healing effects.[23]

Harriet Van Horne guessed at what the message to the country might be: "From Camp David will shortly come another message of inspiration for the American people. The gist of it: 'Sacrifice' . . . What's left to sacrifice?"[24] What indeed? Or, rather, *who* indeed?

On July 15, 1979, President Carter addressed the nation and told them what he had heard on the mountaintop and what he was going to do to relieve our despair:

Fantasy Analysis of
Presidential Address to the Nation
July 15, 1979

Fantasy Words	*Interpretation*
Pain...war...urgency ...blood...sweat...tears ...love...love...neck... stretched...knife...war... war...guns...crisis... erosion...destroy...emptiness...crisis...warning ...shocks...tragedy... bullet...murders... agony...shock... wounds...twisted... pulled...last breath... sacrifice...sacrifice...crying...sweating...war ...war...fight...cut cut...war...fight...sacrifice...attack...rebirth	I know you are in pain, as though you were at war. I know you feel a terrible urgency. You want me to give you blood, sweat and tears so we can love again. Someone will have to have their neck stretched out and a knife used on him. We may have to go to war, with guns, to end the crisis and destroy the emptiness inside us. I am now warning you: there will be shocks, tragedies, bullets, murders, agony. There will be wounds, bodies twisted and pulled, people taking their last breath. There will be a sacrifice. There will be crying and cutting and wars and fighting. If we sacrifice now, we will attack and have a rebirth of America.

The columnists had been right. There would have to be a magical sacrifice by "a tribal shaman who calls on the unseen spirits to work their healing effects." It was the oldest principle of mankind: When the world seems full of guilt, rage and despair, when everything seems polluted and you are certain the end of the world is near, *sacrifice*. For in this sacrifice—whether of animal or human—the group will be purified. Bad feelings will be purged and all bad blood between us will be cleansed.[25] All rage will be vented on the sacrificial object, the group will experience a rebirth and the nation will feel whole and able to love again.

Jimmy Carter knew well the principle of the cleansing power of sacrifice. Like a majority of Americans, he celebrated the sacrifice of Christ for the sake of the world every Sunday of his life. Like a majority of Americans,[26] he had experienced the rejuvenating power of Christ's sacrifice in a personal born-again religious experience. In his July 15th address to the nation, analyzed above, he reminded us of the necessity of sacrifice in bringing about national rebirth. First he described the severity of the emotional crisis: "We can see this crisis in the growing doubt about the meaning of our own lives . . . threatening to destroy the social and political fabric of America . . ." Then he told us the source of our problem, our prosperity: "too many of us now tend to worship self-indulgence and consumption . . . we've discovered that owning things and consuming things does not satisfy our longing . . . piling up material goods cannot fill the emptiness . . ." And finally he promised us that a sacrifice, "a little sacrifice from everyone" would produce the needed "rebirth of the American spirit."

Where, then, might this sacrifice take place? America was, after all, a civilized country, which meant that we would feel guilty about too openly sacrificing our citizens for our emotional needs. It was therefore necessary to set up our sacrificial stage on some foreign soil and to find an "enemy" to take the blame for the sacrifice.[27] Which country was the most likely to respond to our suggestion to become our sacrificial executioner? Which country would we most like to designate as our "enemy"?

The answers to these questions could be found in a Gallup Poll taken in February of 1979. Gallup regularly asks people about the "popularity" of various foreign nations, and the two which had the lowest favorable ratings in 1979 were Cuba (26%) and Iran (27%):

GALLUP POLL: FAVORABLE RATINGS
HOW AMERICANS RATE FOREIGN NATIONS

	1979	1976	% Change
Canada	91	91	even
China (Mainland)	29	20	+ 9
China (Taiwan)	59	55	+ 4
Cuba	26	15	+11
Egypt	63	49	+14
Iran	27	48	−21
Israel	68	65	+ 3
Mexico	72	74	− 2
Russia	34	21	+13

Cuba, of course, was a previous "enemy" of America, and a brief attempt was made by Carter in the fall of 1979 to stir up interest again in Cuba, with a "discovery" that Russian troops were on the island. Yet Cuba, for its own internal reasons, didn't seem interested in being our executioner, so the other unpopular country, Iran, would have to help us perform our sacrifice.

The poll cited above was also important in revealing how Iran had fallen in the eyes of the American public in the previous three years. It is rare for any country to fall 21 points in so short a time. Since the poll was taken in February of 1979, the Shah was still in power, so it was not just "revolutionaries" which were hated by Americans. Later in the year, when revolutionaries took American hostages, tore down American flags and chanted "Death to the Americans" in mass rallies, it became obvious that they were willing to participate in our sacrifice. In the face of these threatening actions, the prudent course for America to have taken would have been at least to beef up our security in Teheran and to avoid taking any actions which might provoke the revolutionaries to take hostages again. Yet, despite repeated pleas for help by embassy personnel, Washington refused to do anything to increase security substantially. So blatant was the invitation to grab hostages that after Iranian mobs had again stormed the embassy, one American general asked in frustration, "How many Americans will have to die before we do anything?"[28]

In June of 1979, *Newsweek* had reported that a White House advisor told them that Zbigniew Brzezinski had said that "a 'small war' might be useful to prove the President's toughness."[29] Obviously, if Iran grabbed American hostages, this might lead to a "small war" which would restore Carter's failing potency and divert the country's rage onto an "enemy" abroad.[30] Though no one said it aloud, the unconscious shared fantasy grew that American embassy personnel would have to be designated as the sacrificial victims. The only problem was to find a way to get Iran to act, and soon.

Despite clear reports from the C.I.A. which bluntly warned that "if the Shah were admitted to the United States, the American Embassy would be taken and it would be a threat to American lives,"[31] important people in America such as Henry Kissinger and David Rockefeller began trying to get Carter to let the ousted Shah of Iran into the U.S. By August, everyone but Carter was for letting the Shah in. American officials in Teheran, slowly becoming aware of their possible role as sacrificial victims, sent an urgent Top Secret message to Washington saying, "The danger of hostages being taken in Teheran will persist. We should make no move toward admitting the Shah until we have obtained and tested more effective guard force from the embassy."[32] Still no additional security was provided.

By October 18th, Carter was the "lone holdout."[33] When his advisers told him he must now let the Shah into the U.S., he bluntly asked them: "When the Iranians take our people in Teheran hostage, what will you advise me then?"[34] There was no question by October that hostage sacrifice was the hidden agenda. The only question was: would the will of the people be frustrated by one lone holdout? Carter would have to be told a lie to get him to cooperate. Although every doctor who had examined the Shah agreed that his jaundice was not immediately serious and could have been treated where he was, in Mexico, and although Rockefeller had sent an American specialist, Dr. Benjamin Kean, to examine the Shah, and he had said that the problem was not life-threatening and he himself could treat him in Mexico, Kean's statement to the State Department was turned into its exact opposite. Carter was lied to by the State Department and told that Dr. Kean had said that the Shah was "at the point of death" and "could only be treated in New York."[35] Carter finally gave in, admitted the Shah into the U.S. for his gallstone operation and the Iranians took the hostages as everyone had predicted they would. America had moved from its third, or "collapse" phase to its fourth, or "upheaval" phase.

The effect on the nation's mood was dramatic. All "collapse" imagery disappeared, and Carter's approval rating in the polls jumped dramatically, as the rage which we had previously directed toward him was now split off and directed toward the Ayatollah Khomeini. *The New York Times* wondered at the reason for this reversal of public opinion,

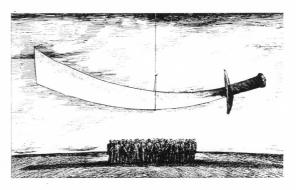

The hostages were pictured as about to be sacrificed.

noting a sudden "deification of Jimmy" and an unaccustomed "hushed reverence" in his presence. *The New Yorker* was puzzled as to why "President Carter's rating of approval . . . doubled during the crisis. The public's sudden rush of affection for its country seems to have included its country's president."[36] At last, we could end our terrible rage against our leader. At last, our ambivalence could be resolved. We had an enemy now to hate, one safely outside our borders. One poll taken during the first week of the crisis revealed how *good* it felt to have an enemy again. The respondents said things like: "We feel unified . . . we can't be pushed around any longer . . . it is good to be an American again . . . my personal life and disappointments didn't seem so important any more."[37] Now all we had to do was complete the sacrifice and have our "small war," and our rage could be vented on the enemy.

In order to give Carter the message that it was necessary to proceed with the sacrifice, tens of thousands of Americans took to the streets to burn Iranian flags, insult Iranians in American colleges, throw rocks

Carter was shown as the all-good leader and the Ayatollah as all bad, with the hostages needed to maintain the split.

through windows of Arab bakeries, parade posters of John Wayne "as a symbol of two-fisted nationalism," and shout "Send in the marines" and "nuke the Ayatollah." As Carter himself put it, "I've got to give expression to the anger of the American people. I guarantee that if I asked the people of Plains what I should do every last one of them would say 'Bomb Iran.' "[38]

Carter was now seen as taking charge of the sacrifice.

Now that Carter had taken charge of the sacrifice, he was pictured in the media as strong and commanding. Iran had, it seemed, saved us from national disaster. "We have been drifting as a country, stumbling along, lacking a sense of destiny," said one person interviewed by *The New York Times*. "Iran could put us back on the right track. Iran has given Americans a sense of purpose, a closeness with the old team feeling that we are in it together."[39] American national unity seemed to depend on the Ayatollah. In fact, if what Iran did made us feel so good, then the Ayatollah deserved our thanks. One columnist said precisely this, in an article which appeared at the end of 1979:

WHY THE AYATOLLAH DESERVES OUR THANKS

The Ayatollah and the street mobs . . . have done this country a hell of a favor. And I don't mean by practically guaranteeing the reelection of Jimmy Carter. The Iranians' contribution lies in prodding the United States into a renaissance of national pride and unity we feared had evaporated . . . [40]

Carter, however, hesitated to take military action, having been informed by his experts that even a successful raid would certainly result in the death of most of the hostages and "hundreds" of others,[41] and that even a "small war" with Iran could equal Vietnam in toll of lives. The nation, its press and its representatives soon grew furious at Carter's delay in moving on with the sacrifice. Newspapers assured him, in front-page headlines, that the lives of the hostages were unimportant because they were aware they had to die: "MARINE HOSTAGES: 'WE ARE NOT AFRAID OF DYING.'"[42] Columnists asked "HOW COME WE DIDN'T DECLARE WAR ON IRAN?"[43] Letters poured in to editors from readers angrily asking why "Carter's all talk and not enough ac-

tion."[44] The Republican National Committee Chairman taunted Carter for his hesitancy, saying he "has engaged in scabbard-rattling in the last couple of weeks, but without anything in the saber [sic]."[45] If Carter didn't act, said *Time*, he would not only be proved

Carter was seen as impotent if he didn't act out the sacrifice.

impotent— he would be like a *weak woman*: "The most dangerous development in world opinion is the growing belief that the U.S. is weak, that it has lost the will to act . . . You don't pick a fight with a man capable of killing . . . Like your wife, America is always around, ready to get a beating."[46]

The real danger, it was soon realized, was the possibility that Carter's patient diplomacy would succeed and the hostages would be released unharmed. If this were to happen, the sacrificial rebirth would be "aborted." William F. Buckley, Jr. summarized this feeling as openly as he dared, with the realization that only if the Americans remain hostages would people be able to be sacrificed:

But what if the Ayatollah merely frees the prisoners . . . The public will be left with a sense of an unconsummated transaction. We will be looking to Carter to see what form he elects for punishing the enduring government of Iran, and here is the rub.

It is unlikely, the hostages having been returned, that the U.S.
will want direct military action of the kind that results in death
for men, women and children.[47]

Most commentators tried not to say openly that the satisfaction of the
emotional needs of the nation required the sacrifice of the hostages. But
many came close to giving away the secret wish behind the growing furor
against Carter's diplomatic route. *The New Republic*, for instance, openly called Carter's statement that he "hoped to secure the release of the
hostages 'without bloodshed' . . . a mistake." The world, it said, was
asking "a dreadful question that is more talked about in private conver-
sation than discussed in print and on the air. It is for how long a nation
places human life, including the lives of its own people, ahead of the national interest and the national repute . . ."[48]

By April, the media reported that most Americans were beginning to
openly call for war and called Carter a coward for delaying: "Seldom has
there been more talk of war, its certainty, its necessity, its desirability . . .
HARLEM KIDS TELL JIMMY TO 'START SHOOTING' . . . The
feeling is widespread . . . that Carter is spineless . . . Carter's 'appease-
ment' is 'even more grotesquely wrong' than Chamberlain's was . . . The
mood in Washington has shifted, from anguished indecision over how to
secure the freedom of American hostages in Teheran, to a seeming deter-
mination to force the issue to a conclusion . . ."[49] After *The Washington
Post* poll showed most Americans now favored using military force
"even if it meant"—that is, unconsciously, *because* it would mean—the
deaths of the hostages, Carter gave the go-ahead to the military "rescue
raid" which his military experts said was bound to result in the deaths of
many if not most of the hostages.[50]

Carter first prepared the nation for the pain that would be inflicted.
The New York Times front-page headline of his March 14th speech read
"CARTER . . . SEES NEED FOR PAIN AND DISCIPLINE," terms
which overtly were a reference to fiscal matters, but which, as with every
message during the crisis, were also understood to apply to Iran. So con-
sistent were the hidden messages during March that in several public lec-
tures and radio broadcasts I predicted that Carter would invade Iran by
the end of April. In one upcoming public lecture I was scheduled to give
at Long Island University on "The Imminent Invasion of Iran"—adver-
tised to take place on April 25th—I warned the sponsor that the events
which I was speaking about might happen somewhere around the day of
my lecture, so that his posters announcing the talk might by then be in
the wrong tense.

At the beginning of April, Carter signalled the Iranians that the sacrifice
would be imminent by giving a speech headlined by the press as
"CARTER SAYS MILITARY ACTION IS THE ONLY CHOICE

LEFT TO U.S. IF IRAN FAILS TO FREE CAPTIVES.'' The Iranian militants received the warning and indicated that they were ready to carry out their part: "IRAN: WE'LL KILL ALL HOSTAGES. The Iranian militants vowed today to kill all 50 American hostages if the U.S. takes any military action. The grim warning came only hours after the White House had broadly hinted that U.S. ships and planes might blockade or mine Tehran's harbor."[52] Everything was set to "lance the boil,'' as Brzezinski put it at the meeting where the decision was made to send troops into Iran.

The "aborted'' military action came the morning of April 25, just hours before my Long Island University lecture, with the result that the audience was considerably confused between fantasy and reality as I spoke, some even charging that I must have somehow participated in the decision to invade the very morning of my talk. Since Carter, to his credit, had refused to send in the vast invasion force which waited in the Persian Gulf, I predicted in the lecture that since he had failed to carry out the sacrifice, our hatred would now return back to him, that he would be defeated by a landslide in the November elections, that Reagan would have to deal with our undischarged rage and that America would finally enact the sacrifice which Carter had failed to carry out by becoming involved in some military action during Reagan's presidency.

After the failed invasion, with eight dead Americans lying on the sands of Iran as further evidence of our impotence, polls confirmed that our

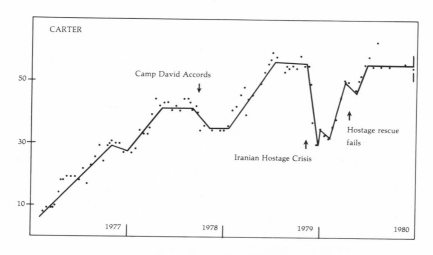

CARTER'S POISON INDEX
Gallup Poll—Percentage of Americans Who Were
Dissatisfied With the President's Performance.

rage toward Carter had returned to pre-hostage levels. Few questioned the likelihood that he would have been re-elected if he had sent in an invasion force and if America had been at war during the election campaign. As one politician put it, "most people would have been grateful to President Carter if he had dropped an atomic bomb on Teheran. He would have been reelected."[53] If Carter couldn't carry out the sacrifice, if he was unwilling to purge us of our national rage, he would have to be

After the failed sacrifice, Carter was pictured as too weak to fight.

replaced by someone who could. As Richard Nixon put it, "One of the major errors that President Carter made [was] that his primary, and in

America felt poisoned by its undischarged rage.

fact it seemed to me his only concern . . . was the lives and safety of the hostages."[54] A leader who refuses to carry out the necessary sacrifices to remove the emotional pollution of the nation leaves us, in the words of one reporter, "choking,"[55] awash in our own poisonous rage. Carter would have to be replaced by someone who *would* carry out the sacrifice and remove our fantasied national poisons.

It would take a modern Hercules to cleanse our Augean stables of so much poisonous rage. It would take a man who could be hard, who this time could wield the sacrificial ax without flinching. It would take an old-fashioned American,

Reagan was pictured as a cowboy hero gleefully killing weak Jimmy Carter in a landslide.

born in an earlier era than Carter and raised in an earlier, more violent, family atmosphere. It would take a man like Ronald Reagan, who could embody our delusion that our pleasures were sinful and our rages justified. It would take a leader who, frightened about his own manhood, would move decisively to military action when we began calling him a weakling. It would take a man who could promise us, as he did in the fantasy language of his acceptance speech, that he knew how we felt and how to provide the sacrificial rebirth which we wanted:

> destroy...disintegrating...weakened...calamity...sacrifice...
> destroy...rebirth...eaten away...wasted away...renew...renew...
> sacrifice...flows like a mighty river...harm...injure...turned the
> national stomach...destroy...freeze...exhaustion...destruction
> ...weakness...disasters...weakness...war...war...war...blaze in-
> to life.

3

THE MAKING OF A FEARFUL LEADER
"Where's the Rest of Me?"

When Ronald Reagan wrote his autobiography in 1964, he entitled it *Where's the Rest of Me?* in order to indicate, he said on the opening page, that he had lived most of his life with the feeling that part of him was missing.

The moment when he felt most acutely that part of him was missing, he wrote, was in 1941, during the filming of the motion picture, *King's Row*. The first description he gives in his autobiography is his growing terror while making the film.

> My key scene was to be played in a bed. This environment was the result of the plot which had me injured in an accident in the railroad yards. Taken to a sadistic doctor (who disapproved of my dating his daughter and felt it was his duty to punish me), the doctor had amputated both my legs at the hips.
>
> It was the portrayal of this moment of total shock which made the scene rough to play. . . . A whole actor would find such a scene difficult; giving it the necessary dramatic impact as half an actor was murderous. I felt I had neither the experience nor the talent to fake it. I simply had to find out how it really felt, short of actual amputation.
>
> I rehearsed the scene before mirrors, in corners of the studio, while driving home, in the men's rooms of restaurants, before selected friends. At night I would wake up staring at the ceiling and automatically mutter the line before I went back to sleep. I consulted physicians and psychologists; I even talked to people

who were so disabled, trying to brew in myself the cauldron of emotions a man must feel who wakes up one sunny morning to find half of himself gone.

I got a lot of answers. I supplied some more for myself. None of mine agreed with any of theirs. Theirs did not agree with each other. I was stumped. I commenced to panic as the day for shooting came nearer.

The night before I could not sleep. I appeared wan and worn on the sound stage, still not knowing how to read the line. Without hope, with make-up pasted on and in my nightshirt, I wandered over to the set to see what it looked like. I found the prop men had arranged a neat deception. Under the gay patchwork quilt, they had cut a hole in the mattress and put a supporting box beneath. I stared at it for a minute. Then, obeying an overwhelming impulse, I climbed into the rig. I spent almost that whole hour in stiff confinement, contemplating my torso and the smooth undisturbed flat of the covers where my legs should have been.

Gradually the affair began to terrify me. In some weird way, I felt something horrible had happened to my body. Then gradually I became aware that the crew had quietly assembled, the camera was in position, and the set lighted . . . There were cries of "Lights!" and "Quiet, please!" I lay back and closed my eyes, as tense as a fiddlestring. . . . I opened my eyes dazedly, looked around, slowly let my gaze travel downward. I can't describe even now my feeling as I tried to reach for where my legs should be. "Randy!" I screamed . . . "Where's the rest of me?"[1]

That the "sadistic doctor" had cut off the legs of his daughter's boyfriend as punishment for his sexual desires was made explicit in the movie,[2] so it was understandable that the scene could be an upsetting one for an actor to play. Yet the portrayal of the punishment of a young man by a father figure for his erotic wishes was hardly a unique theme in the theatre. Why did having to say a single line throw Ronald Reagan into such a "panic"? What personal meaning did it have for him that he chose to use it as the title of his autobiography, that he referred to it hundreds of times in his speeches since then, and that he even asked to have the movie's theme music played at his Presidential Inauguration? Why has it been so difficult for him to separate himself from the movie character who screamed out "Where's the rest of me?"

From the description he gives of his emotions during the filming of the scene, it appears that for some personal reason he was unable to separate the portrayal of this "castration" scene before the cameras from his own castration fears. Yet to say he had "unconscious castration fears" is only to begin to understand why he was so panicked by the scene. Every man, to some degree, has unconscious castration fears, and every woman, to some extent, fears of body mutilation. What must be asked is what was special about Ronald Reagan's life to that point which might make him so identified with the movie character who had his legs cut off? What family background, what personality development and what circumstances in his life in 1941 can help explain why this one line has remained identified in his mind with his self-image for the rest of his life?

From a look at Reagan's career, it soon becomes evident that the castration theme has always been a major concern of his. To begin with, he often refers to himself as "bleeding," from his oft-repeated description of himself as once having been "a hemophilic liberal—I bled for 'causes' " to his regular use of such phrases as "I bleed real blood for the unemployed" and "no fighter ever bled as I did." Even his favorite childhood poem contains the bleeding image in its opening line, "I will lay me down for to bleed a while." Sometimes this preoccupation with himself as bleeding expresses itself in the negative, as after the Carter debate, when he said to a reporter, "I've examined myself and I can't find any wounds."[3] But usually his castration imagery is overt, references to the "cutting and slashing" of "hemorrhaging budgets" having been part of his political language since the beginning of his career.

Typical Reagan doodle shows himself with hands and legs missing.

The castration anxiety shown in his choice of language extends to his drawings. Although Reagan is an excellent graphic artist, he has difficulty in drawing hands, legs and horse's hooves in his sketches and doodles. Most of his drawings show his preoccupation with castration in some way, and his self-portraits usually come out looking like graphic illustrations for the "Where's the rest of me?" scene, with his hands and legs often missing.[4]

In addition to just his choice of words in his speeches, Reagan will often work open references to mutilation into conversations, usually in connection with the issue of capital punishment. For instance, when he became Governor of California in 1967, he refused to give clemency to Aaron Mitchell, a black man who had been given a death sentence for having shot a policeman during a robbery. When asked by a group of civil libertarians why it was necessary for Mitchell to die, he startled them with a detailed, graphic description of "one of the most macabre cases in California annals . . . which involved the sexual mutilation of the male victim,"[5] even though the mutilation case was totally unconnected with Mitchell. A few days later, in a speech before the National Sheriffs Association, he changed to a graphic description of the bloody mutilation of a ten-year-old girl, who, he told the sheriffs, "had been stabbed 60 times and had been mutilated in a savage and depraved manner,"[6] again a case unrelated to the topic of his speech. The reason he related the story, he told his listeners, was to show that sexual mutilations were so commonplace that misdeeds must be followed by "punishment immediate and certain."[7]

The original version of this dreaded sexual mutilator who so haunts the life of Ronald Reagan, the childhood source for his overly severe castration fears, was his father, John Edward Reagan. This connection is shown by the fact that immediately after relating the "Where's the rest of me?" scene in his autobiography, Reagan turns to his relationship with his father and his father's life-long alcoholism. Even though Reagan always tried to avoid talking about his father to interviewers—one biographer said that when asked about his family life he would "talk nonstop about his mother" but never mention his father[8]—he relates in the autobiography how as a child he would be "pretending sleep" during his father's "week-long benders," and how he would "fill myself with grief for my father" when he found him "spread out as if he were crucified" on the front porch.[9] The father, a violent Irishman, who was later described by his son as having lived a life of "almost permanent anger and frustration,"[10] used to kick young Ronald "with his boot" and often "clobbered" him and his brother.[11] From even the few memories which emerge in his scattered comments about his father, it is evident that Ronald's relationship was filled with frequent episodes of terror and a longing for closeness, feelings which he shared with many others of his generation (he was born in 1911) due to the generally much harsher childrearing practices then common.[12]

His overwhelming fear of his father made young Ronald a "good" boy, a "loner," who was "afraid of the dark," someone who suffered since childhood from various phobias, or irrational fears of various kinds.[13] The first phobia he mentions in his autobiography is his fear "to the point of hysteria" of being piled upon by "the mass of writhing, shouting bodies" in a football game.[14] Although he always loved the physical violence of football—enjoying the "clean hatred . . . where two men can literally fling themselves bodily at one another in combat"—he said he always panicked when he felt trapped by the pileup.[15] His claustrophobia, his fear of being trapped in an enclosed space, was a "lifelong" problem, he told one biographer.[16] Most of the time it indicated fears of physical closeness, usually with men, as when he had a "claustrophobia problem" when filming a movie in a submarine in close quarters with other male actors.[17] Other phobias would be temporary, depending on his life situation, as when he was afraid to fly during his eight years of speaking engagements for General Electric, when he had to write a clause into his contract guaranteeing his travel would be only by train,[18] or as in his avoidance of New York restaurants because the tables were so "close together . . . your shoulders are virtually touching the fellow's shoulders at the next table."[19]

In all cases, however, Reagan's phobias are similar in purpose to those of other phobics in helping him to avoid any situation which might lead to a loss of control over his feelings, positive or negative. This avoidance is necessary whenever any situation might tempt him to express emotions of love or hatred too directly, and thus invite punishment by "the father in his head," his extremely severe conscience.[20] Reagan shares with others who have phobias the fear of loss of control and the over-concern about humiliation and being made to feel worthless, situations which might force him to show his rage and invite punishment, symbolically, by castration.

Phobias are one of the most thoroughly understood neurotic symptoms, going back as far as Sigmund Freud's accurate analysis of a phobic in his early work, *The Interpretation of Dreams,* an analysis which has a direct relevance to Reagan's phobias and even provides a clue to what was really going on in the crucial scene in *King's Row.* Freud says:

> I had an opportunity of obtaining a deep insight into the unconscious mind of a young man whose life was made almost impossible by an obsessional neurosis. He was unable to go out into the street because he was tortured by the fear that he would kill everyone he met. He spent his days in preparing his alibi in case he might be charged with one of the murders committed in the town. It is unnecessary to add that he was a man of equally high morals and education. . . . After his father's painful illness and death, the patient's obsessional self-reproaches appeared—he was in his thirty-first year at the time—taking the shape of a phobia transferred on to strangers. A person, he felt, who was capable of wanting to push his own father over a precipice from the top of a mountain was not to be trusted to respect the lives of those less closely related to him; he was quite right to shut himself up in his room.[21]

Freud's account provides the solution both to Reagan's phobias and to the mystery of his castration anxieties during the "Where's the rest of me?" scene. First, we must take into account Reagan's personal circumstances during the filming. He had just gotten married, in January of 1940, and had just had his first child, Maureen, in January 1941, both dangerous actions on his part, revealing that he had sexual wishes and inviting punishment from his father. Then—though this date is mentioned neither in his autobiography nor in any of his biographies—his father died four months later, on May 18, 1941.[22] Like Freud's patient, Reagan felt that ever since he was a child and was kicked and beaten by his father, he had wished for his father's death. When his father *really* died, in 1941, Reagan unconsciously felt *he* should be punished, as the *King's Row* character was punished. During the filming, a few months after his father's death, when he found he had to portray a scene showing that his legs had been cut off, he panicked. It was too real, an almost exact duplication of his personal situation at that time. When he looked at the flat covers "where my legs should have been," he "felt something horrible had happened to my body" because he felt *he himself* deserved castration, for marrying, for being sexual, for becoming a father himself, for having wanted his own father dead.

After the death of his father and the making of *King's Row*, Reagan went into the army. When he got out, his personal life quickly began to slide downhill. He first spent six months doing nothing but building model boats. Then he went back to work in such a depressed mood that he spent most of his time quarreling with his studio and avoiding his wife, Jane Wyman, by spending all his free time at Screen Actors Guild meetings. His need to sabotage his marriage soon became so severe it led to a divorce. In the court proceedings, Jane Wyman stated that the marriage had ended because his union activities took all his time. But perhaps more to the point was her remark to Gregory Peck, after the hearings, that the reason why she left Reagan was that "I just couldn't stand to watch that damn *King's Row* one more time."[23] Reagan obviously had continued to be obsessed by the castration scene, viewing it repeatedly in an attempt to master its personal meaning for himself.

By 1947, Reagan's despair about his life reached its climax. He began carrying a loaded pistol—ostensibly, he said, as protection against mutilation threats,[24] but also as a return to his earlier having owned guns as a child and in his twenties.[25] He let his physical condition run down so badly he came down with pneumonia, went to the hospital and became aware that he wanted to die. While in bed, he hallucinated that Humphrey Bogart was in the room with him (Bogart was a father-figure to him at that time.) He describes the hallucination in his autobiography:

> Humphrey Bogart appeared, and we played an interminable scene exchanging and wearing innumerable trenchcoats, and trying to say lines to each other, always with a furtive air of danger in the surrounding darkness. Someone else can take a crack at analyzing what this Freudian delirium meant. This was evidently the night—"Big Casino, bet or throw in." . . . I decided I'd be more comfortable not breathing.[26]

Reagan had become so depressed, he felt he wanted to "exchange trenchcoats with Bogart"—that is, exchange places with his dead father (trenchcoat = shroud). His guilt at outliving his father, his conviction that his wishes had actually killed him, had grown to such a point that only the ultimate punishment, his own death, would suffice. At that moment on the hospital bed, he was thrown back to his childhood, when he sometimes used to feel so depressed that he wished for death, once writing a poem extolling death as a salvation from "life's dreary dirge."[27] If a devoted nurse had not coaxed him to continue breathing, he said, he would have quit living then and there.[28] Something would have to change in himself if he was to go on living with his guilt.

What Reagan changed was his life goal itself. After his pneumonia episode, he suddenly decided to become an anti-communist. As for many Americans, anti-communism was for Reagan a perfect solution for his parricidal wishes. It solved the problem of his guilt for his father's death by putting his disturbing wishes into the communists. Without being consciously aware of why, he found that his new anti-communist activities made him feel better, saying to himself, in effect, "It's not *me* who wants to kill daddy. It's *the commies* who want to destroy all authority. And if I fight *them*, I'll be able to control *my own wishes in them*."[29]

His conversion from acting as a career to being an anti-communist politician was, Reagan said, like finding "the rest of me," like moving from a "monastery" into a life of action.[30] Now, rather than accepting the self-image of a passive boy, guilty of his father's death, he could assume the active role as a fighter against those who want authorities dead. Rather than staying at home and endlessly watching himself on the screen without legs, he could—like FDR, another man who had used politics to conquer the loss of his legs—take action against those who now embodied his dangerous wishes. The moment he switched from being a liberal Democrat to a crusading anti-communist, he not only found the rest of himself, he solved the problem of guilt in his life, by taking all the things he felt guilty about and putting them into an "enemy." At the age of 36, Ronald Reagan had finally found how to live without crippling anxieties.

His new defensive mechanism even enabled him to remarry without conscious guilt. In marrying Nancy Davis, he was able to repeat the crucial mutilation scene from *King's Row* . . . except that this time the outcome was one of triumph rather than defeat. Nancy's father, like the sadistic father in the movie, was also a surgeon, and Reagan made sure he repeated the film's scenerio as closely as he could by arriving for their first date on crutches, having broken his leg in a baseball game.[31] This time, however, he could marry the surgeon's daughter because he was able to externalize his guilt for his sexual wishes by putting his guilt-provoking wishes into the communists, "the most evil enemy mankind has known in its long climb from the swamp."[32]

For Reagan not only saw communists as parricides, but also as extremely active sexually—completely in contrast to the actual sexual code in most communist countries. For instance, when he ran for Governor of California, one of the central themes of his campaign was "the mess at Berkeley," a place where, he said, they held "sexual orgies so vile I cannot describe them to you," promising if elected to "investigate the charges of communism and blatant sexual misbehavior on the Berkeley campus."[33] A good part of the reason why he was elected was that, as one biographer put it, "hidden away in the hearts of parents was the fear that their own children might one day go away to college, grow beards and march against authority."[34]

Reagan promised these voters that his first targets as Governor would be the students at Berkeley, "advocates of sexual orgies, drug usage, and filthy speech," who wanted only to "disrupt the academic community" and who therefore must be brought under control immediately.[35] The situation at Berkeley, he told a woman's club in April of 1966, was now so bad that their "morality gap is so great that we can no longer ignore it." He had proof, he said, that the Alameda County District Attorney had just investigated a student dance which had turned into "an orgy," where they had displayed on a giant screen "pictures of men and women, nude, in sensuous poses, provocative, fondling."[36] Since Reagan had waved a piece of paper in the air during the speech, saying that he had the report of the DA's investigation "in his hand," curious reporters later asked the DA for a copy, only to be told that "my office made no investigations of the college dance."[37]

This typical incident illustrates one of the problems with using politics as a way of solving internal problems. For those who externalize their own anxieties, action is more often taken to solve current personal problems than to deal with actual situations in the real world. A vast gulf separates the anti-communist crusade of Reagan and others and rational actions taken to reduce real threats by communists and others. The crusading anti-communist sees dangers *when his or her own feelings are about to get out of control* rather than when reality is actually becoming dangerous. Orgies at student dances could hardly be considered one of the major dangers to the State of California in 1966. Reagan's political actions are far more likely to stem from current dangers in his own inner life than from dangers in the real world. Because of his severe personal problems—ones which he shares with many Americans—he is likely to overlook reality conditions which need attention in favor of situations which represent wishes of his own which are giving him problems.

When Reagan needs to dump his wishes into others, it often leads him to actions which violate his own conscious sense of fairness. For instance, one month after Reagan became Governor, he received a $2 million gift from Twentieth-Century Fox, disguised as a payment for some land he owned which had cost him little and which was so "barren and craggy," according to *The Wall Street Journal* article revealing the affair, that the county real estate appraiser said the sale was obviously "not a fair-market sale." The president of Fox's real estate unit told a reporter who later asked about the incident, "Why should we want to air those dirty linens? It would just dirty Fox's name. Maybe management decided they owed Reagan a favor. Who knows? Who cares?"[38]

Whatever the motives behind the $2 million gift and whatever its connection to the real-estate backers who had asked Reagan to run for Governor, the money made Reagan rich for the first time in his life. But the satisfaction of such forbidden wishes made him feel guilty. Someone would have to be punished for his own greedy wishes. Part of that "someone" turned out to be needy and retarded children. The very same day that Reagan received the $2 million gift from Fox, he was drafting a budget which increased his own pay and that of other state executives, but which also cut out virtually all funds for the Needy Children's School Lunch Program and which also cut the 79 cent a day meal allowance for retarded children in state mental hospitals. The allowance contained a main meal, before the proposed cut, which was described as "watery navy beans, cole slaw, one thin slice of bologna dry around the edges, one slice of bread and a cup of milk."[39] That Reagan felt bad about having to cut the 79 cent meal allowance of retarded children was obvious from his defensiveness about the cuts, claiming that they would actually "improve" the meals.[40]

Now Ronald Reagan was clearly not personally cruel toward children in his life. Even though he distanced his own children somewhat by sending them to boarding schools, he was certainly not abusive toward them. He even gave money for the poor to charity every year. How, then, could he cut a 79 cent a day meal allowance for handicapped children?

The answer to this recurring puzzle—as always when public action deviates so markedly from private morality—is that once a personal defense system is established which depends on dumping disavowed feelings into political objects, people no longer have a conscious choice over their actions. Those weren't *real* children who were being made to suffer, they were *symbols*, symbols of Reagan's own "greedy" desires. The children's very real suffering *had* to be denied because the children contained *parts of Reagan* which he had to disown. His own personal feelings toward children were secondary. He had to cut the 79 cent meal allowance in order to punish "the greedy child in himself" for having become so rich. Only by punishing an appropriate scapegoat could he feel relieved. The retarded children just happened to be one of the appropriate scapegoats available.

This mechanism extended to all of his budget-cutting efforts. That he was little interested in actually reducing the total expenses of the State of California was obvious from the fact that the state budget more than doubled during his term. Real budget control is a tedious, demanding job, one which requires real expertise, which Reagan was uninterested in acquiring. Yet because he himself had become a rich and powerful man, he—like so many rich and powerful people—had to advocate a rhetoric of asceticism in government in order to still his own guilt about his personal condition. That he mainly chose to cut budgets for the poor and helpless—symbolically, children, symbols of his own childish wishes—made little difference to his surface political image as a budget-cutter. In fact, hidden beneath this surface image was the known fact that he was actually a big spender, who at the same time could be counted on to sacrifice the poor and helpless as magical guilt-reducing devices.

Government, to Reagan—as to many of his supporters—was not seen as an adult, helpful or harmful as the case may be. Government was a place where one could dump one's childish wishes and then attempt to control them. "Government is like a baby," he said, "an alimentary canal with an appetite at one end and no sense of responsibility at the other. If you keep feeding it, we'll be up to our neck in something . . . oh yes. Debt."[41] Government is the place we put our "greedy baby" wishes, and if we feed them, we'll drown. Government, like the communists, is "the enemy," and it is a mistake to think it might help people. As Reagan put it in his campaign, "The time has come for us to stop being our brother's keeper."[42] Even if one *becomes* the government, one must deny it. "We belong here only so long as we refer to government as 'they' and never think of it as 'we,' " he told his staff after taking office.[43]

Once Reagan dumps his dangerous feelings into the political arena, his central problem is to bring under control situations which threaten to get "out of control." As he puts it, those who support him agree with his deepest feelings that there is "a panic fear in the air, partly due to a feeling of helplessness, a feeling that government is now a separate force beyond our control . . ."[44] The more his disturbing inner feelings could be injected into the political scene, the better he felt—even if to an outside observer the situation hardly seemed something to feel good about. For example, students were easy to provoke in the Sixties, and thus were excellent containers for his inner rage. Therefore, as one of his biographers, Bill Boyarsky, put it, "As governor, Reagan used to *revel* in confrontations with students."[45] The more chaotic the situation on

California campuses, the happier Reagan appeared to feel. In 1969, during the student riots in which Reagan would blurt out his famous statement that "if it's a blood-bath, let it be now," a typical work day was described as follows:

> Then he prepared a statement, called a press conference a day ahead of schedule, and told hastily assembled reporters he was proclaiming a state of emergency and calling out the California Highway Patrol to protect the university from "criminal anarchists" and "off-campus revolutionaries." "Students have been assaulted and beaten as they attempted to attend classes," Reagan said. "Streets and sidewalks providing access to the campus have been physically blocked. Classes have been disrupted. Arsons and fire-bombings have occurred and university property has been destroyed." Reagan was happy about what he had done, saying to his press secretary, Paul Beck, on the way back to his office, "I'll sleep well tonight."[46]

In contrast to the night before the *King's Row* filming, when he "could not sleep" because he was trying to deal with chaotic feelings *inside* himself, now he would "sleep well," because the chaos was safely *outside* himself.

Unfortunately, this process of dumping internal problems into the political arena is only effective if the people around the leader share his delusions on some level and agree to help him control his feelings. As one author puts it,

> persons with anxieties create an atmosphere of anxiety around them and feel better if this anxiety is outside themselves. This also may have a double-edged character; if they succeed too well, and discover that everyone around them is really frightened, they may feel they have destroyed their potential protection, are endangered by retaliation, and suddenly become extremely frightened themselves.[47]

The formula "turmoil outside equals peace inside" therefore has its limits, for Reagan as well as for others like him who use politics to solve personal problems. When they finally make everyone around them so frightened that the outside world no longer seems able to safely contain their disowned feelings, the situation is suddenly then seen as terribly threatening. In order to restore their inner balance, they may then have to take violent action to destroy "the enemy" who now seems to be "out of control."

It is precisely at this point where the personal psychology of the leader intersects with the shared fantasies of the nation. When the nation feels "strong," during the honeymoon period early in the leader's term of office, people idealize him and tell him how wonderful his programs will turn out. He is convinced that he can keep the nation (and his own dangerous wishes) "under control" through his ability to sacrifice such groups as "welfare cheats" and others who are imagined to contain all the nation's bad, "greedy" wishes. But when these minor sacrifices appear to fail, when the leader appears to be weakening and the nation "collapsing," the leader unconsciously feels it is *his own personal dumping process* which is getting "out of control." He then is tempted to imagine an "enemy"—generally foreign—who is "on the move." What is newly threatening, of course, is *internal*; it only appears to be external. But it seems to be terribly dangerous just the same.

That the dangerous "enemy" is in fact our own feelings is our most deeply denied truth. Yet it is made obvious by the unnoticed fact that we never go to war in the first year of a presidency, only when our leader's authority appears to have collapsed.[48] This "collapse" state has no actual relationship to reality conditions, only to internal shared fantasy states. Most of the "dangerous" periods in our history have been based on fantasy, not reality. This is particularly true of our anti-communist fears, beginning with The Truman Doctrine, which was proclaimed in 1947 when America enjoyed an atomic monopoly and Russia lay prostrate from World War II damage, but which Dean Acheson nevertheless saw as the time of greatest threat to America in our entire history.[49] These "collapse" fears soon led to the bloody, protracted Korean War against communism. This was followed by the generally peaceful and less fearful Eisenhower years, when—although in reality Russia had gained enormously in military strength and nuclear missile development—we felt for internal reasons much less threatened. So, too, the inner feelings of "collapse" during the turbulent Sixties , which led to the Vietnam War, had their origin more in our own internal state of mind than in anything which had happened in Asia.[50]

There are times of growth and stability when the nation chooses a personality like that of Eisenhower, who would in the middle of a crisis go out to putt on the White House lawn, saying to reporters that "the mere fact that some little incident arises is not going to disturb me. I have been scared by experts, in war and in peace, and I am not frightened about this."[51] There are other times, in reaction to a period of rapid economic growth and important personal and social change, when America chooses a personality like that of Truman or Johnson, both of whom share with Reagan a need to inject their personal desires into outside "enemies" in order to control them.[52] This explains why, when Reagan first began to run for the presidency, in 1975, his candidacy produced little response from a nation busy revitalizing its economy, expanding its social welfare programs and changing its family and work conditions through major women's rights and sexual revolutions. The second time around, however, in 1979, the nation, reacting to the vast changes produced by the previous four years, was in a different mood altogether. When Reagan announced his candidacy this time, despite one observer's worries that "a man approaching seventy is going to have a hard time giving a new speech when he's given the same speech two hundred nights a year for twenty years,"[53] America was in a completely different mood. This time, we *needed* someone who mirrored our inner anxieties about the personal, economic and social changes which had so much affected our lives. This time we needed Ronald Reagan.

The mood of the nation after the anxiety-producing changes of the Seventies—and after Carter had refused to purge these anxieties through a large-scale Iranian invasion—was summed up by Henry Kissinger in the fantasy language of his Keynote Address to the 1980 Republican Convention:

> weakness...impotent...upheavals...disaster...painful...fear
> ...slid...shocked...chaos...feeble...fear...upheaval...paraly-
> sis...humiliation...disaster...slipping...weakness...crash...
> fears...whipsawed...unraveling...impotence...chaos...des-
> pair...crushing...turmoil...lost...disasters...war...impotence
> ...war...war...fears...dark forces

No greater contrast could be imagined between this language of "disaster" and "humiliation" and the hopeful feelings of the 1976 Democratic Convention which had nominated Jimmy Carter. The nation was now looking for an entirely different kind of personality, someone who could reflect their sense of "impotence" and "chaos," someone whose personal problems forced him, like the nation, to see "turmoil" and "dark forces" where none existed. During the campaign, Carter's restrained personal style was simply overwhelmed by Reagan's flood of castration language emphasizing "bloody cuts," "despair" and "pollution." The contrast can clearly be seen in their respective responses to the questions put to them in their October 28th television debate.

Carter-Reagan Television Debate
October 28, 1980
Fantasy Words

Q: War? Paralysis? Cuts?

R: Heart...falls...war...war
...wars...bleed...bloody
...cuts...cuts...cuts...cut
...cutting...war...cut

C: Injection

Q: Shocks? Shock? Cutting? Cut?

R: Plague...cut...lick...
grinding...flood-
ing...cutting...wiping out
...cuts

C: Cut

Q: Deterioration?

R: Bombed-out...great
gaunt skeletons...
smashed out...despair...
bulldozed down...bully...
dead...witch doctor...
burn...clean...pollution
...pollution...rug pulled
out...frighten...destroy
...roof fall in

C: Despair...deteriorating
...sex...purity...eggs...
pollution

Q: Weakness?

R: Misery...misery...heart
...lonely...off the backs
...turn loose

C: War...war...weakness...
war...lonely

Try as hard as he could, Carter could not match Reagan's deep feelings of death, despair and destruction. An ABC poll found Reagan the winner of the debate by a 2-1 margin.[54] We had found someone who felt about himself what we felt about ourselves, someone who agreed that the changes of the past decade had made everything seem to be "out of control," someone whose monetary policies promised to provide us with scapegoats who would be punished for our desires. For most of Reagan's actual abilities mattered little to us—that because of his emotional problems his grasp of reality was so damaged that he was a poor administrator, that he knew little about economics, that his phobic work habits were so poor that he had to be fed digests of complex problems on one-page summaries and fell asleep at important meetings whenever he felt too trapped by their intimacy.[55] Nor were his considerable personal charm and his ability to communicate on television important in producing his landslide election victory. What elected Ronald Reagan was two promises he made to us:

(1) that he would bring to a halt the growth and disturbing changes of the Seventies by producing a recession which would sacrifice people who were appropriate symbols of our greediness, and

(2) that if this internal sacrifice should fail to make us feel better, he, unlike Carter, could be counted upon to provide us with an external sacrifice, a military action which would at last give us an object for our rage and wipe out the "enemies" who represented our dangerous wishes, the communists.[56]

With these crucial unconscious promises uppermost, Reagan's America could begin to accomplish the historical task of the early Eighties: what to do with the anxieties produced by the new vision of personal and social life that had evolved during the Sixties and Seventies.

4

REAGANOMICS AS A SACRIFICIAL RITUAL
"Cut, Slash, Chop"

The scene is a familiar one for most psychotherapists. The patient tells the therapist in his initial interview what he believes is his main problem: "I seem to be unlucky with women. I've been married three times, and each of my wives left me for another man. And now my girlfriend has just left me too. How can I stop women from being unfaithful to me?"

Therapists hear similar complaints daily. "All my boyfriends treat me like dirt." "I keep running into bosses who do nothing but fight with me." "Every career I've tried is boring." "None of the women I meet want to get close." Faced with such repetitive life patterns, one of the hardest tasks of the therapist is to point out to the patient that their major complaint is also their major wish—that they unconsciously *choose* unfaithful wives, uncaring boyfriends or hostile bosses in order to avoid the anxiety aroused in themselves if they were to enjoy their families, love lives or work too much.

Imagine, then, how difficult it becomes to analyze a *nation's* psyche. Imagine Uncle Sam on a couch, describing what he believes to be his main problem: "I seem unable to enjoy a really sustained success at anything. I keep getting into periods of depression during which I lose much of what I've worked so hard to gain. Why, in this century alone, I've gone through twelve major cycles of boom and bust, and I seem condemned to repeat the pattern endlessly. And to top it all off, just as things seem to be looking up, I get involved in a war that puts me even more behind, so that I'm now over a trillion dollars in debt. How can I stop my bad luck?"

If this were the complaint of an individual, the therapist would not hesitate to diagnose a "success neurosis," a "manic-depressive pattern" which the patient unconsciously brings about in order to limit the anxiety aroused by success through periodic self-destructive acts. Yet it seems to go against conventional wisdom to entertain the notion that our collective life might be an extension of our individual lives, with repetitive patterns brought about by unconscious wishes. Despite the astonishing regularity of business cycles (every eight years on the average for developed countries)[1] and of wars (every twenty years on the average for most nations),[2] they have never been considered as *wishes*, ways of limiting the anxiety caused by the enjoyment of our lives through periodic self-destructive scenerios which we ourselves carefully stage. Like the patient who sees his problems as the result of "mistakes" in his life, conventional wisdom sees economic and political crises as the result of collective "mistakes," whether they be "mistakes of overinvestment," "mistakes in fiscal policy," "mistakes in the money supply" or "the mistakes of Munich." Business cycles and war cycles are rarely seen as being motivated.

The reason social problems so often seem to be a result of mistakes is that most social analysis has been based on a model of "economic man," who is seen as acting in his or her own self-interest, maximizing pleasures, working rationally, spending wisely and saving prudently. This assumption requires that one overlooks the embarrassing fact that those whom one knows personally resemble the model of "economic man" very poorly if at all. One's neighbors seem often to spend unwisely, save little, have work difficulties or drink excessively, or are too depressed or too timid or too rigid or too bored or too angry either to fully use their talents or to really enjoy their family lives. In reality, people are every bit as irrationally human as current novels report them to be, and are more likely to fit a model which shows them as *limiting* their pleasures and abilities than as maximizing them. Even those who do manage to experience success at work often seem to end up either disliking what they do or sacrificing their family lives or love lives or health "to their jobs." People who are psychologically healthy enough to succeed and enjoy their work *and* their possessions *and* their families *and* their sex lives turn out to be rare indeed in the real world.

But if most individuals limit their satisfactions and sacrifice their talents, earnings and pleasures so as not to provoke too much guilt from excessive enjoyment of living, so too must *nations* made up of these same individuals do so. A sound theory of psychoeconomics must therefore include an investigation of the various strategies by which nations engage in *surplus destruction* as well as surplus creation—strategies which include periodic booms, busts and wars.

Contemporary economists occasionally stumble upon the possibility of self-destructive motivations, but since their model only allows "economic man" to be rational, they dismiss the notion as obviously too crazy to entertain seriously. Often one reads authors who, after attempting to explain business cycles according to rational models, find them so insufficient that they throw up their hands and say, as does Paul Samuelson, that it almost seems as if people "wantonly pursue a manic-depressive pattern and thereby create the business cycle,"[3] or, as does Robert E. Lucas, Jr., that one is tempted "to suggest that people *like* depressions."[4] But the authors quickly back away from their momentary psychological insights and return to their basic model of rational "economic man" and his unmotivated "mistakes."

The most obvious place to observe these self-destructive acts in operation is in primitive groups, which spend much of their time destroying their surplus in sacrifices to their gods. In fact, the reason that contemporary primitives have remained at a low technological level is precisely because they have continued for millennia to sacrifice their surpluses, while more advanced groups long ago began to allow their surpluses to accumulate and produce economic progress.[5] The consciences (superegos) of primitives are so severe—due to their poor childrearing practices[6]—that they rarely allow themselves to own anything as individuals. What they produce, they do so mainly for the group as a whole. Reciprocal gift-giving rather than individual ownership and trade is the main basis of their economic systems. What surplus they manage to accumulate during the year they destroy in yearly sacrificial rituals "to the gods" (to their severe consciences), burning, consuming or otherwise destroying surplus food and goods to prevent their guilt from building up. The annual sacrifice of these goods becomes a ritual of revitalization of group life, a way to clean their psyches of the accumulated guilt produced by the surplus-building efforts of the previous year.[7]

For example, the Northwest Coast Kwakiutl Indians accumulate a rich supply of animal and fish all year long. By the end of the year they feel so guilty about their surplus that they halt all economic activity for several months while holding complex Winter Ceremonials in which their stated aim is to compete to see who can give away and destroy the most food and goods. The individuals who destroy the most surplus receive the most prestige, because they contribute most to "taming the Man Eater," the god who wants to "swallow wealth."[8] At the Winter Ceremonial, a dancer portrays the Man Eater, and the central myth that is enacted in the ritual is the feeding of food, goods and even corpses to the voracious, devouring mouth of the god.

Kwakiutl Indians bring up their children very severely, tying up (swaddling) their babies for three years to "control their appetites," harshly weaning them and teaching them every minute of their lives that their desires are bad and that if they dare to enjoy anything they risk turning into cannibal-children. It is not surprising that when these children grow up they become adults who are afraid of their every impulse, and instead put their repressed desires into the outside world, which is then seen as being "filled with mouths . . . a world filled with omnipresent man-made images whose mouths betray their greed."[9] It is this world of hungry mouths, of monstrous appetites—ultimately, of their own hunger for love—which must be "tamed" at their annual cannibalistic rituals.

So, too, in other primitive groups, the guilt which is built up during the year is cleansed through the annual destruction of the group's surplus, through a "feeding of the gods," a "taming" of each individual's own devouring wishes, while destroying the surplus which produced the guilt in the first place. Different groups accomplish this periodic sacrifice in different ways. The African Ankole "feed" cattle, milk, grain, beer and even humans to their Royal Drum, which is the container into which they inject all their poisonous devouring wishes.[10] The Ashanti have a "Golden Stool" which acts as a similar poison container. The Baganda have a "King's Placenta" which accomplishes their cleansing ceremonies. In Dahomey, the king sat on a giant platform, and the entire country would cleanse the evil spirits in their midst by "feeding the king" with cattle, food and cowrie-money, gifts which they believed physically carried the poisonous pollution (their own feelings), which only the king could cleanse.[11]

Primitive cannibalistic rituals were seen as necessary to "tame the Man Eater," our own appetites.

When primitive groups meet more advanced people and dramatically increase their goods, they also invariably increase their sacrificial efforts to destroy their new surplus and avoid the guilt brought about by their unaccustomed wealth. Thus, early in the twentieth century, when the Kwakiutl met the white man and increased their prosperity a hundredfold through trade, they simultaneously increased their Winter Ceremonials, transforming what originally was a modest sacrifice of goods into a massive ritual where thousands of blankets and other valuable objects were given away, burnt or thrown into the river in order to "tame" their newly-provoked desires.[12] In addition, when surplus increases, sacrificial warfare also increases. By the time a group reaches the level of a kingdom, what was at an earlier level only small raiding parties evolves into the organized warfare of early states, involving virtually continuous warfare with tens of thousands of professional soldiers.

The Aztecs, for example, sacrificed to a sun-god as their "Man Eater," and since their childrearing allowed them to build up more surplus than their earlier forebears, their sun-god had to contain an enormous amount of their greedy desires. Their "Man Eater" was seen as so voracious that it had to be fed real blood to satisfy its appetite, and every man, woman and child would regularly draw blood from their thighs, arms and genitals to "feed" to the sun (their own severe consciences) to prevent it from becoming angry and plunging the world into darkness.[13]

Yet even regular contributions of blood by the people did not satisfy the sun-god's appetite, so ritual human sacrifice on a huge scale was practiced by the Aztecs, in which the still-beating hearts of captives were torn from their chests and fed into the sacrificial fire to "renew the vitality" of the group. Huge piles of skulls were arranged on a rack near the temples to show the gods how many

The Aztecs sacrificed humans to feed the sun and quench its appetite.

victims the group had sacrificed lately, and the priests and others would emulate the sun's appetite for human flesh by eating portions of the people who had been sacrificed.[14] War, too, served the blood thirst of the gods. Young men, pledged since birth to die and give their blood to the sun, vied for the honor of sacrificing themselves on the battlefield.[15] If the usual wars with neighbors did not suffice to feed the gods enough blood, the priests would complain to the army, and volunteers would march out to a nearby battlefield, divide up into equal groups and slaughter each other until the gods were finally satisfied.[16]

Despite all this sacrificial activity during the year, the wealth of the Aztecs continued to increase, and so did their guilt. Every 52 years,[17] therefore, their sun-god would become so polluted with the people's poisonous guilt feelings that the end of the world would threaten. Time would stop, the sun would die and a new sun would have to be born to prevent the gods from descending and eating up every last Aztec on earth. The New Fire Ceremony which accomplished this periodic major guilt-cleansing was the Aztec's most sacred ritual. All economic activity would slow to a halt during this dangerous time, and the priests would mount a hill, carrying a distinguished warrior for sacrifice. Just as the night grew darkest, as the sun sank deepest, perhaps never to return, the priests would rip out the heart of the victim and offer it to the fire-god. In the victim's chest cavity where his heart (the old sun) had been, the priests would place a sacred fireboard. A new fire would be lit in the chest cavity, symbolizing the birth of the new sun. This fire would then be used to re-light all the sacred bonfires in the kingdom, and people who saw them would rejoice because they knew the sun had died and been reborn, cleansed of pollution through human sacrifice.

It is only by using a model of society based on the shared fantasy of a dying sun and of the periodic sacrifice of the few in order to cleanse the feelings of the many that the policies of Reagan's America can be understood.

Reagan pictured as head priest to a Volcker-god who demands human sacrifices.

Blood Shortage

The Federal Reserve was seen as needing the blood of all Americans.

In this model, the role of the chief sacrificial priest was taken by Ronald Reagan, and that of the sun-god, the blood-thirsty idol of the temple—the Man Eater, complete with sacrificial fire and bones of victims—by Paul Volcker, Chairman of the Federal Reserve Bank. The ''economic crisis'' which Reaganomics was designed to cure was, like that of the Aztecs, seen as a condition of moral pollution, as a shortage of blood (investment capital) and as a time when everything was "out of control." Only a "Time of Sacrifice" was believed to be able to tame the appetite of the gods (our own feelings) and allow us to be reborn and cleansed of our guilt for the surplus of recent years.

It was the major task of Reaganomics to provide America with this Time of Sacrifice. This would be accomplished by slowing down the economy through bleeding our life-blood (our money supply), by frightening the people (with high interest rates and huge deficits), by vastly exaggerating dangers (of inflation, of debt, of the strength of enemies) and by welfare cuts and planned unemployment which sacrificed symbols of our desires (women, children, the poor, the unemployed.) If our Time of Sacrifice was successful, the guilt-producing surplus of recent years could be drained away (the polluted blood cleansed), the upsetting social changes of recent years could be reversed (our sinful excesses expiated) and we could allow a rebirth of our economic sun by releasing once again the supply of money and credit, rejoicing that the spectre of too much pleasure had been averted and the body politic had been purged of its impurities. This cleansing function of Reaganomics was in fact so paramount that it included the building up of a huge new war capacity, anticipating that if the internal sacrifice of victims of the recession did not suffice to make us feel

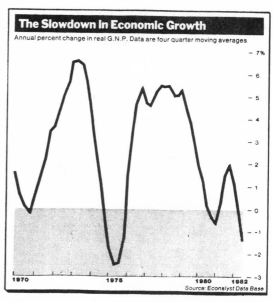

Reaganomics had to plunge the economic sun below the horizon for a Time of Sacrifice.

better, we, like the Aztecs, could move to an external sacrifice, a military encounter, which could provide us with additional sacrificial victims.

It must not be imagined that phrases such as "the victims of Reaganomics" are purely metaphorical. An effective sacrifice requires a real Man Eater and real deaths. It is not too difficult to determine the approximate number of additional deaths brought about during Reagan's Time of Sacrifice. A careful statistical analysis has been made by the Congressional Joint Economic Committee of the average increase in mortality rates during recessions for suicide, homicide, cardiovascular deaths and other indices of mortality affected by economic activity. Extended to the present period, these rates show that approximately 150,000 additional deaths can be attributed to the effects of Reaganomics.[18] To this figure must be added the deaths attributable to Reagan's budget-cutting efforts—mainly those aimed at the tens of millions of women and children helped by government programs—such as the deaths

Women and children were seen as good sacrificial victims.

caused by the reduction in child nutrition programs, in Aid to Families With Dependent Children, in nutrition programs for low-income pregnant women, in the Federal School Lunch Program, in funds for handicapped children, in disability benefits and so on. The direct cutting of such aid easily pushes the death toll for Reaganomics far over the

Three million children were cut from the school lunch program.

150,000 figure.[19] Finally, this figure does not include the indirect deaths produced by such effects as the reduction in environmental protection enforcement, cuts in aid to philanthropic organizations, including UNICEF, the loss of health insurance by millions of unemployed workers, the deaths in underdeveloped countries affected by the Reagan recession and many other similarly lethal actions.

That the Congress which passed the Reagan program so willingly during his early months knew full well that these 150,000 dead men, women and children were being sacrificed on the economic altar is clear. As Rep. Phil Gramm, co-sponsor of Reagan's budget bill, put it at the time of its passage, "We are shooting real bullets."[20] That we, too, knew at some level the lethal effects of Reaganomics is also clear. We laughed at the comedian David Frye when he impersonated Reagan by saying that he had "found a way to reduce our over-population without abortion—by increasing our suicide rate" because in our hearts we knew that we ourselves had hired the priests who would preside over the Time of Sacrifice. When 1981 polls showed 70 percent of Americans felt that Reagan's economic program was "fair and equitable," we were saying we approved of this sacrifice of over 150,000 men, women and children.

Although it is difficult to believe, *many of those sacrificed to Reaganomics approved of the sacrifice.* The following *Washington Post* survey of the victims of Reaganomics, taken in 1983, summarizes the feelings of those out of work, those whose families were ill and could not be treated because of lack of medical insurance, those whose lives were ruined by the Reagan recession:

> We don't blame you [Reagan] for the recession. We'd gotten too fat, too comfortable, too uncompetitive. Our standards aren't as high as they used to be and there's plenty of blame to go around . . . Besides, we still believe in those Puritan values you talk about. Perhaps we had to suffer to purge ourselves of our excesses.[21]

All modern nations go through a similar Time of Sacrifice every eight years or so, in as inexorable a drama as the periodic sacrificial rite of the Aztecs. The phases of the business cycle are quite thoroughly understood by economists. Only the motivations have remained unexplored. There are three major phases in each cycle, depending upon the changing attitudes of people toward work and pleasure. These are *The Time of Work, The Time of Mistakes* and *The Time of Sacrifice*.

The Time of Work begins when, after the purging of guilt of the previous recession, people feel for a time that they now are allowed to innovate, invest, work, spend and even enjoy the fruits of their labors. The new innovative activity is led by a minority within the nation, a new, more optimistic "psychoclass," people who have been brought up somewhat more lovingly and less afraid of their impulses than the rest of the nation.[22] This new psychoclass is able to expand the nation's production through new products and new processes undreamed of by the older, more repressed psychoclasses. The Time of Work—whether it be the New Era Prosperity of the 1920s or the New Frontier and Great Society of the 1960s—uses the full resources of the nation, expanding production without producing inflation and spreading prosperity to more of those at the bottom of the economic ladder.

Within a few years, the growing guilt of the majority of the nation (especially the older psychoclasses) about this wide-based prosperity soon produces a Time of Mistakes, when nothing seems to go right. This phase begins a two-stage manic-depressive cycle, as nations—exactly like individuals who are manic-depressive—first try to ward off their guilt about too much success by "manic" activity. The "mistakes" include overspending, unwise investments, inflationary wage demands and pricing policies, overextensions of the money supply and credit structures, overstocking of inventories, real estate manias, foolish loans abroad and a whole range of ways of getting rid of the guilt-tainted surplus. Economic historians who study this phase of the business cycle are puzzled as to why so many mistakes are suddenly made by so many sections of the economy. In some nations, where most of the people have been brought up very strictly—such as in Weimar Germany—the manic printing of money can produce a hyperinflation so severe that all money becomes worthless. The economy then grinds to a halt, removing the guilt, and the government can then "rectify its mistakes" and stop the thousands of printing presses from working overtime.[23]

The third phase of the business cycle, the Time of Sacrifice, is usually seen as a reversal of the manic, or inflationary, phase, but it actually is a *continuation* of its guilt-reducing process, only now all economic activity is "depressed" rather than wildly sped up. A fantasy is shared during this phase that things had gotten "out of control." The nation is imagined to be a giant body with two parts: a top, which must be fed, and a bottom, which must be punished. The role of the top part of the body is taken by the rich, and the fantasy is the familiar "trickle-down theory"—that if the rich are fed, the poor might somehow benefit. It is the same fantasy expressed by the primitive Anyi of Africa, when they used to say as they brought gifts to their king and his court in time of trouble, "When the king's breasts are full of milk, it is his people who drink."[24] All "supply-side economics" is based on this magical fantasy, whether carried out by David Stockman in the 1980s or Andrew Mellon in the 1920s. What we wanted was to "let the hogs feed," as Stockman phrased it,[25] to make the rich fatter, under the delusion that we were all infants dependent upon their maternal breasts for our sustenance.

That the "supply side" argument for feeding the rich—supposedly as a way to increase investment—was thoroughly irrational was revealed by studies made by the Federal Reserve Bank, *Business Week* and others[26] which showed that America's investment rate was actually at its highest in decades, that there existed "a record $80 billion pile of ready cash" available for investing whenever the demand existed and that money shifted to the wealthier part of the nation at the expense of everyone else would only dry up demand further and produce *lower*, not higher, investment. Few were surprised, then, when, as the Reagan plan took effect, investment *plunged* rather than rose. "Supply side" tax cuts for business and the wealthy had only *felt* right; few claimed it could be *demonstrated* as right. As Senator Howard Baker admitted when he passed the program, "What we're doing is really a river boat gamble . . . we're gambling that this new economics will work."[27]

The other task of the Time of Sacrifice, that of "punishing the bottom," involved a similarly delusional fantasy shared by most of the nation—that we were bad in enjoying so much prosperity and that part of us must suffer for our badness. Just as when we were children it was our bottoms which had to be punished, so too the bottom half of the body politic—the poor, the unemployed, women and children on welfare—would have to be punished for the indulgences of the rest of us. The first thing which was necessary was to strangle our economic bloodstream, our money supply. We suddenly "discovered" monetarism and reversed the growth of our monetary supply, "bleeding" our economic system of its life-giving blood, precisely as doctors used to bleed their patients to remove the "polluted" blood which they imagined had been produced by "overindulgences in food and sex."[28] It was, of course, not just a "mistake" for the Federal Reserve Bank to allow too much money in the Seventies and then suddenly to squeeze the money supply so hard that interest rates went to 20 percent and no one could buy cars or houses. It was, rather, the *purpose* of the Fed to produce these erratic swings in money supply, in accordance with the manic-depressive cycle. If they hadn't done so, we would never have had a Time of Sacrifice, and within a few decades our steady growth in productivity would soon have produced so much surplus that everyone in America would be living comfortable, and we would have no poor whom we could make suffer for our guilt.

In a similar vein, it is only when the sacrificial, "purging" nature of Reaganomics is taken into account that what seemed to be its conflicting parts can be viewed as a coherent whole. It has often been demonstrated that the two parts of Reaganomics—monetarism and "supply side" tax cuts—don't make sense hitched together. Economist James Tobin states the case clearly:

> The idea that money and prices can be detached and delegated to central bankers while Congress and the executive independently take care of budget, taxes, employment and output is the kind of fallacy that makes exam questions for freshman economics, a fallacy now elevated to presidential doctrine. If Amtrak hitches engines at both ends of a train of cars . . . one engine heading west to New York, the other east to Boston, and advertises that the train is going simultaneously to both destinations, most people would be skeptical. Reagan is hitching a Volcker engine at one end and a Stockman-Kemp locomotive to the other and telling us the economic train will carry us to full employment and disinflation at the same time.[29]

What Tobin overlooks is that providing a train with two engines going in different directions is a plan *designed to produce a train wreck*, i.e., purposely set up to reduce surplus, sacrifice productive capacity and provide victims of the crash. The "supply side" tax cuts of Stockman were the "feed the rich" fantasy and the monetarism of Volcker was the "punish the poor" fantasy. Reagan implemented both at the same time as a way of insuring the sacrifice of the minority to relieve the conscience of the majority. The only question which remained was, as Stockman told one reporter, "How much pain was the new President willing to impose?"[30]

When Stockman put his budget figures into the computer and found that even with the most optimistic assumptions Reagan's actions would produce deficits in excess of $100 billion, he told the *Atlantic Monthly* reporter that he found the figures "frightening—'absolutely shocking,' he confided—yet he seemed oddly exhilerated by the bad news."[31] Why "exhilerated by the bad news"? Because he knew we had hired him to produce bad news, to produce a Time of Sacrifice, to produce 150,000 victims.

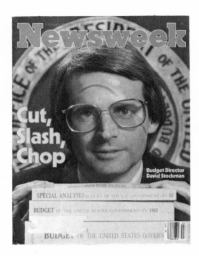

David Stockman was assigned the job of chief executioner who would "cut, slash and chop" the victims.

Similarly, the huge rise in defense spending—$1.6 trillion in five years—complemented rather than contradicted the other parts of the Reagan program, because it, too, destroyed surplus which we otherwise might have enjoyed. Military spending solves a crucial problem of post-World War II economics of nations. Since childrearing has improved since World War II, nations in the West have recently replaced Great Wars and Great Depressions by limited wars and limited recessions. The result is that, in America, our real Gross National Product since World War II has jumped by over 30 percent a decade, a prosperity so unprecedented that if it continued unabated it could soon do away with poverty for good. One way we have found to prevent this from happening has been to pour $2 trillion into the military since World War II, using up resources which, if they had been put instead into new technology, would have given America a productivity rate far exceeding even that of Japan (which accomplished its "miracle of modernization" simply by spending very little on their military.)[32]

This "disinvestment" strategy of ensuring low productivity by draining resources into military expenditures is further sustained by the shared fantasy of most Americans that the Man Eater—the International Communist Serpent, really our own projected feelings—was growing and was about to devour us at any moment. By the time of Reagan's election, after the prosperity of the Seventies, fully 71 percent of Americans said we must spend more for the military.[33] That this involved an enormous increase in useless and highly dangerous

Reagan's task was seen as "taming the Man Eater" through budget cuts and military buildup.

military expenditures—almost a billion dollars a day, every dollar of which is drained from our present or future pleasures—is not a *drawback*. It is an unconscious *purpose*. An extra billion dollars a day in pleasure would simply be intolerable to our puritanical consciences.

It cannot be emphasized too strongly that it was pleasure which was the enemy that Reaganomics was designed to defeat. It is no coincidence that the bible of Reaganomics, George Gilder's *Wealth and Poverty*, was written by a man who had become famous writing anti-feminist books opposing the sexual revolution, saying that men have been "cuckolded by the compassionate state" which had encouraged women's sexual and career independence to such an extent that a man could "no longer feel manly in his own home."[34] The enormous anxiety felt by men of the older psychoclass about the sexual freedom of women cannot be overestimated. Earlier in the century, the average American woman rarely had orgasms and wanted sex only once or twice a month.[35] Today, women not only have sex much more often, but are so open about their ability to enjoy it that young women wear T-shirts saying "God, it feels good" . . . an attitude toward pleasure which cannot help but produce anxiety in the older psychoclass.

The puritanical counterattack of the Reagan team against the sexual revolution is consonant with their sacrificial economic program of "feed the rich" and "punish the poor." When Gilder was asked by an interviewer whether it wasn't true that "the rewards of supply-side economics are given right now, to the wealthy" while "the penalties are imposed right now, on working-class, low-income, welfare citizens," he replied, with a grin, "That's life, folks."[37] And when his fellow "supply-sider" Jude Wanniski called his Reaganomics team "the wild men" who fought against "the forces of darkness,"[38] it was the "dark force" of sexual pleasure as much as it was the pleasure of consumption which was being combated.

The gratitude felt by most Americans toward the man whose task it was to bring the dark forces of our pleasures under control was overwhelming. Washington had never seen the likes of the $8 million Inaugural Celebration, supplemented by 40,000 guests attending "satellite balls" across the country. *The New York Times Magazine* ran a front cover instructing Reagan on his regal task, with the following headline: "MEMO: TO THE PRESIDENT. What this country wants and needs is not a board chairman or a passive

The Reagan Revolution was seen as opposed to pleasure.[36]

President, but a strong one, even—yes, even—something approaching the old and besmirched Imperial Presidency."[39] Those who wondered if all the ostentation of the ten-thousand dollar gowns and the $1,000-a-plate new dinnerware wasn't perhaps an inappropriate way to begin the cutting of the budget for the poor didn't really understand both halves of the principle of "feed the top and punish the bottom." Reaganomics needed *both* the golden presidential plates *and* the welfare cuts to carry out its fantasy.

The overt adulation of the country toward Reagan personally knew no bounds during his first year. *Time* made him "Man of the Year." *The New York Times* thought he was simply radiant: "Mr. Reagan is the first President in years who seems comfortable in the public eye, and he is radiating charm, decency—and competence."[40] *The New Republic* agreed that he shined all over: "Reagan is direct, simple and sincere—candor shines out all over him."[41] TV reporters saw him as a messiah who would reverse our disastrous past, as Jimmy Carter had promised but had failed to do: "After 20 years of pessimism, after assassinations, Vietnam and Watergate, at last, the burden was off our backs. It was America Reborn, a New America, America All the Way!"[42]

Swept up by the nation's adulation, Reagan's team could proceed with the sacrifice of the 150,000 people with dispatch. David Stockman found out "how much pain the new President was willing to impose" simply by listing program after program to be eliminated or drastically reduced, each with a little box for Reagan to check—something like the Roman system of sacrificing Christians in the Colosseum. The victims would ascend the sacrificial ladder each time a box was checked. One observer, present during the procedings, told of the ease with which the sacrifice was carried out: "Reagan, this insider says, would look at the proposal, glance around the cabinet room table, and say, 'Well, is there any disagreement on this one? No? OK, that's done, let's go on to the next page.'"[43] Each stroke of the pen, like an executioner's ax, struck a blow against the symbols of our excesses. "Cut," down go 3 million children removed from the school lunch program. "Slash," down go 340,000 CETA jobs for unemployed workers. "Chop," down go the handicapped children helped by government aid. It was as easy as cutting the 79 cent food allowance had been in Sacramento. In fact, it was even more important for Reagan personally to cut the budget for children now. When he had become Governor, he had just been made a

Reagan was seen as being in charge of the government guillotine.

millionaire, and he had sacrificed the needs of a few thousand children as symbols of his "greedy" desires. When he became President, he had deposed the former President (a father-figure), had himself taken over as the most powerful man in the world and now ate off thousand-dollar plates. Millions of children would now have to suffer for the *hubris* of his daring.

Even stopping the nation's money supply growth wasn't difficult for Reagan, despite the supposed independence of the Federal Reserve Board. "It took only one visit at the end of April 1981, when President Reagan finally called Volcker to the White House and in no uncertain terms asked Volcker whether he intended to control the money of America . . . the Fed officials froze money growth for six months to October 1981, thus precipitating the current recession."

One after another the victims of Reaganomics ascended the sacrificial ladder.

What's more, adds the reporter, "The President should have pinned Volcker's ears back long before April 1981."[44]

That Reagan could perform his sacrificial role so effortlessly while still being thought of as "charming" and "nice" is more a testament to our desire to delegate to him the unpleasant sacrificial role than to any innate "charm" in his personality, which could be quite prickly when opposed. During the passage of the budget bill, House Speaker Tip O'Neill said of Reagan, "He's cutting the heart out of the American dream to own a home and have a good job and still he's popular."[45] He might more accurately have phrased it *"Because* he's cutting hearts out, he's popular." Given our euphoric idealization of Reagan in his sacrificial role, it was comparatively easy for him to implement his program. Despite *The Washington Post*'s quite accurate statement that "Reaganomics . . . never was taken very seriously by the bulk of the economics profession,"[46] the *public* took it very seriously indeed.

As soon as the President's program passed Congress, the stock market dropped. Despite Reagan's magical scenario about the revitalization of America which would result from the sacrificial cleansing of the body politic, Wall Street knew precisely how bad the Time of Sacrifice would be. Despite $143 billion worth of tax reductions for business depreciation,[47] and despite slashes in corporate tax rates, they knew that profits were nevertheless going to drop sharply while Reagan pushed the economy down to a utilization rate of below 70 percent which would be required to destroy some of the surplus of recent years. Although businessmen would not have to actually lose their lives as would the 150,000 human victims of Reaganomics, they would have to do without some of their profits for a while as their contribution to the Time of Sacrifice.

Nor did the Democratic party oppose the sacrificial slaughter. The few who noticed that the work of decades was being dismantled were reduced to impotence within the party. "It's heartbreaking," said one. "We

Both parties asked Reagan to chop off heads.

spent years putting those programs together, and they work. Now they are being destroyed."[48] "People are watching programs they have put their hearts and sweat into being cut and abolished," said another. "They're walking around in shock."[49] Democrats played key roles in passing every part of the Reagan program. As one Republican said, "Without them, we could not have won."[50] Appropriately, they were labeled "Gypsy Moths" and "Boll Weevils," devouring insects, symbols of the devouring, biting mouths of the Man Eater to whom their victims were being sacrificed. As one *New York Times* editorial put it, they "were victimized last week not so much by a Republican man-eater as by Democratic boll weevils."[51] As in the world of the Kwakiutl, Reagan's America seemed to be filled with biting mouths, "Republican man-eaters," "Gypsy Moths," "Boll Weevils," and millions of hungry mouths in the Pac-Man games which swept the nation at that time.

The other symbol used regularly in these early months came right out of the pages of Reagan's autobiography, *Where's The Rest of Me?* Since Reagan's main fear was of castration, of losing his legs, every slash of the budget ax gave him a chance to prove that he was able to do to others what he feared his father had wanted to do to him. Everyone around him joined him in the use of castration imagery during the budget-cutting process. Rep. O'Neill said his hope was that budget cuts for the needy would be modified so as to "cut them off at the knee instead of cutting them off at the hip."[52] An Education and Labor Committee aid said, when informed of the cuts, "It's like being told to amputate your own leg."[53] Reagan himself regularly used the phrase: "Vote against me, and you will cut me off at the knees."[54] When Reagan finally signed the budget bill at his California ranch, a reporter asked him to hold his leg up in the air, ostensibly to see his new boots. The resulting photo of

Ronald Reagan displays his powerful phallus after signing the sacrificial legislation.

Reagan, laughing, with his leg high in the air, was run in almost every newspaper and magazine in the nation. He *did* have a powerful phallus after all. He *showed* it to us. It was the *victims* of the bill he had just signed who were castrated, not Reagan. The scenerio from *Where's The Rest of Me?* was so much on everyone's mind during the signing ceremony that as the meeting broke up, after Reagan had displayed his leg, a reporter asked him what he was going to do next. He replied:

PRESIDENT: "Go out and cut the brush."
REPORTER: "Well, don't cut your leg off."
MRS. REAGAN: *"Where's The Rest of Me?"*
PRESIDENT: "You shouldn't have mentioned it."

The castrated had become the castrator. The child once sacrificed to his father's rage had become the sacrificer. This time, America had chosen the leader it needed. After feeling "out of control" for so long, it felt good to be in control again.

5

CARRYING OUT THE SACRIFICE
"Laser Eyes"

Actually carrying out the sacrifice would not be an easy task. When Ronald Reagan declared in his first address to the country that "the American economy was in the worst mess in half a century," real Gross National Product, total industrial output, total jobs and real personal income were the highest of any nation in history. The only sense in which America could have been considered to have been in "the worst mess in half a century" was because of our overwhelming guilt from such unparalleled prosperity. Given the extraordinary vitality of the American economy, Reagan's main problem was to find ways to halt the growth of this prosperity for a couple of years while sacrificing symbols of our greedy desires in order to cleanse us of our guilt. This would not be a simple task.

What would help Reagan most in slowing down the economy would not be just the power of the government, as important as that was. Even more useful would be the shift to puritanical attitudes by most of the country as he came to office. The resurgence of puritanical strictures against enjoyment could be seen everywhere at the beginning of the Eighties, not just in the extremes of the Moral Majority. "New TV Season: Sex Is Out, Old Values In," *U.S. News* accurately proclaimed,[1] and the same was true for the movies, beginning already with *Star Wars* and *Superman*, both based on traditional heroic scenarios. The ethos of the Eighties preached hardness and viewed pleasure as weakening, an attitude by itself guaranteed to reduce spending.

To back up the shift to the new puritanism, new myths had to be invented. For instance, "permissive attitudes toward sex" were held responsible for what was thought to be an "epidemic of teen-age pregnancies," in order that sexual freedom for teenagers could be attacked. That the actual statistics showed teenage pregnancies steadily declining since 1957 (from 96 per 1,000 to 53 per 1,000 by 1980) was conveniently ignored.[2] Even many liberal educators shared this shift to puritan attitudes. As just one example, Dr. Sol Gordon, the founder of National Sex Education Week, whose books had been instrumental in opening up sex education for teenagers, now proclaimed that the "recent increase" in teenage pregnancies was "a national social disaster." "I can't think of any good reason for teenagers to have sex," he told the American Association of Sex Educators, Counselors and Therapists. "Sex is a health hazard to boys and girls."[3] The same sort of conservative shift was evident in all areas of American life, as the older psychoclass reacted negatively to the freedom and prosperity of the previous two decades.

Given this puritanical mood, the people of America were, if anything, ahead of Reagan in his early months in their demands that something be done quickly to reduce American prosperity. When he still hadn't passed his sacrificial budget by the summer of 1981, his Gallup disapproval rating (poison index) began climbing at a faster rate than any previous president's in American history. He would have to move fast if he were to prove to us he could be a successful sacrificial leader.

By early summer, Reagan's media imagery had moved from "strong" to "cracking," months earlier than Carter's, and he had to admit at his June 16, 1981 press conference that "we are seeing the first beginning cracks"—ostensibly in the Soviet empire, but really in his own image. Something would have to be done soon to assure the people that he was, indeed, determined and ruthless enough to carry out the internal sacrifice . . . and, if necessary, the external sacrifice as well. This "something" took the form of two carefully-staged actions designed to convince the country that he could carry out sacrifices. These actions were (1) the destruction of the Professional Air Traffic Controllers Organization (PATCO), and (2) the shooting down of two Libyan jets.

Reagan moved to the "cracking" stage earlier than Carter.

We thought that Reagan was weakening.

The firing of the PATCO workers, termed "an ambush" by one neutral observer,[4] was set up by Reagan's letter of October 20, 1980 to Robert Poli, head of PATCO, promising him, in return for his election support, that he would back PATCO's demands and "will take whatever steps necessary . . . to adjust staff levels and work days commensurate with achieving a maximum degree of public safety." In the next six months, Reagan's negotiators encouraged PATCO to believe that they were open to union demands and that a strike could be part of the bargaining process, only then to have Reagan summarily dismiss the 12,000 PATCO members and bankrupt the union because they went out on strike. According to one Presidential aide, Reagan "wanted to jut his jaw out . . . He wanted to be tough." The action was applauded by almost everyone in America, from the whoops of joy in the business community for "finally sticking it to the unions" to the two-to-one margin of approval by the public in the Gallup poll and *The New York Times* editorial which called the firings "a commendable precedent." Precedent it indeed would be, but mainly for a ruthless attitude toward workers in the recession, not for union-busting.

The carefully-staged destruction of PATCO even impressed the Kremlin. According to Richard Pipes, Reagan's advisor on Soviet affairs, "Seeing photographs of a union leader being taken away in chains—that surprised them and gave them respect for Reagan. It showed them a man who, when aroused, will go the limit . . ."[5] Back in 1970, when the postal workers struck, they were rehired. But this was the Eighties. This time, as *The New York Times* reported it, "the White House leadership team, smiling and joking among themselves, looked on at 11 A.M. Monday as Mr. Reagan announced his deadline and brushed aside suggestions that his first move toward the controllers might have been less severe. 'What lesser action can there be?' he said, his face expressing amazement."[6]

Equally staged was the shooting down of the Libyan jets a few weeks later. Libya's leader, Muammar al-Qaddafi, played a very special psychological role for the Reagan period—that of Reagan's "evil double." When cartoonists and others wished to portray elements of the repressed, "out-of-control" sadistic image of Reagan, they often drew a Qaddafi figure using a familiar Reagan symbol.[7] For instance, Qaddafi was shown swinging a sacrificial sword—Reagan's most often-used symbol during his first year—with sadistic glee and lots of blood, even

though the real Qaddafi had no connection with swords. Like all split-
off feelings, our attitude toward
Qaddafi was thoroughly irrational.
He was not just the leader of a small
country. He was something very
close to our hearts—evil per-
sonified, "a cancer which has to be
removed," according to Secretary
of State Alexander Haig.[8] The
Qaddafi-devil symbol would play an
important role whenever America

**Qaddafi was pictured as swinging
Reagan's sacrificial sword.**

needed a figure of pure evil for group-fantasy purposes, a place to put
our own sadism.

Qaddafi was therefore chosen as an appropriate target for Reagan's
first foreign killing. The Libyan shootdown was as carefully planned as
the PATCO firings. Although in 1980 Jimmy Carter had avoided
holding Sixth Fleet maneuvers in the disputed Gulf of Sidra waters near
the Libyan coastline, Reagan knew that in order to have a shootdown he
would have to provoke the Libyan planes patrolling close to the shore.
The operation was staged as carefully as a Hollywood movie. First, the
exercise was moved from July, when the Defense Department had
originally planned it, to August, to avoid media conflict with Reagan's
budget victories. Next, Reagan personally gave instructions for the
American planes to shoot down the Libyan planes, since the Navy's standing rules of engagement often allowed them to ignore confrontations
such as these.[9] White House technicians then installed extra media equipment and phones in Los Angeles, where the President would be staying
during the shootdown, in order to be able to handle the extra teletype
and phone traffic that would result. A week before the exercise, the
White House encouraged *Newsweek* to run a feature article describing
the coming "testing" of Qaddafi, giving the Libyan leader plenty of
notice that he was being challenged. As the F-14 Tomcats headed toward
the Libyan coast on August 19, they met two Libyan SU-22 jets. Both
sides said the other fired first. The superior American Tomcats quickly
destroyed the Libyan planes, as planned. At least one of the Libyan
pilots died in the shootdown. It couldn't have been more successful.

Reagan had staged the incident so carefully he wasn't even awakened
when the planes were shot down. Unexpectedly, this led to media
speculation that he was not "in control" of the shootdown—whereas he
was actually more like the director of a thoroughly-rehearsed stage play
who didn't come to the opening. Reagan laughingly admitted later that

he already knew when he went to bed the battle was going to take place: "If our planes were shot down, yes, they'd wake me up right away. If the other fellows were shot down, why wake me up?"[10] The staged quality of the whole event was so flagrant that, according to one reporter, "When he saw his top assistants for the first time the morning after, Reagan performed a bit of pantomime, impersonating a Western gun-slinger drawing six-shooters from both hips."[11] Again, he was John Wayne. Finally, as planned, he went to have his picture taken wearing a "Commander-in-Chief" cap aboard the aircraft carrier *Constellation*, watching Navy planes being launched, giving the impression in the media that he had been physically present during the Libyan shootdown.

The meaning of the shootdown was understood by everyone in America. As Ed Meese put it, "We're not going to war. We're just shooting 'em down."[12] It was our first taste of blood under Reagan, wholly unnecessary for any diplomatic purposes, but vital as a question put to the American people as to whether it would be allowable to attack small nations in the future in order to make us feel good. The media answered with an exultant "Yes." *Time* thought killing Libyans was fun: "A YANKEE DOODLE DAY: Victory In The Air, Fun At Sea . . ."[13] The *Daily News* headlined Reagan's boast: "RON ON LIBYAN INCI-DENT: 'WE'VE GOT THE MUSCLE.' "[14] The *New York Post* saw the attack as having shot down Reagan's critics:

DOGFIGHT BLASTED REAGAN'S CRITICS

President Reagan's closest advisers believe last week's inci-dent off the coast of Libya should quiet those critics who charge the Administration has failed to articulate a foreign policy. "That dogfight did for us what 20 presidential speeches never could," a high ranking official said.[15]

In the press conference on the shootdown, Secretary of Defense Weinberger and General Gast of the Joint Chiefs of Staff had to lie about the planning for the incident, claiming that "no specific instruc-tions" were given to shoot—but they nevertheless looked so jubilant that one reporter was moved to ask, "You said that they carried out their mis-sion extremely well. It seemed as though you are almost proud of the way . . ." Weinberger interrupted testily, "I don't think it's necessary to try to do any amateur psychoanalysis at this time."

Like the PATCO firings, the shootdown of the Libyan planes was crucial to our group-fantasy aims. It was the revenge of the old psychoclass for relative American restraint and resulting humiliation in Vietnam and Iran. And it was a promise for the future, accomplished in a meaningful way, through *action*, "better than 20 presidential speeches.'' The major media carried no protests about the shootdown. Both sides of the political spectrum applauded Reagan for his ''decisiveness and strong leadership,'' and for his quick action, so different from Carter's civilized restraint. *Time*'s Hugh Sidey, a Reagan supporter, reported that ''Pollster Richard Wirthlin last week hustled his latest sampling out to Reagan in California. It showed deepening support across the country—a feeling that Reagan's recent actions, from his victory over the air controllers right up to his air victory over Libya, have clearly been in the national interest.''[16] The *Los Angeles Times'* Charles William Maynes, a Reagan critic, agreed it was good to attack small targets: ''You don't have to agree with the Reagan Administration's overall approach on key issues to admire its tactics . . . It moves decisively when the target is small, unpopular and manageable. Both the continuing conflict with the air controllers and the new crisis with Libya, different as they are, fit this pattern.''[17] Political commentators instinctively connected the PATCO and Libyan shootdowns, as though by those two symbolic actions during the months of August 1981 something important for America had been decided. They were right. Reagan felt it in his body when he impersonated John Wayne the gunslinger, shooting from the hips. Since in politics the most important communications are conveyed in symbolic action rather than in words, the two incidents were questions from Reagan to the American people, and our praise for both actions was our answer, our authorization for more of the same in the future. The destruction of PATCO authorized the internal sacrifice, and the Libyan shootdown authorized the external sacrifice. Now we *really* were Reagan's America, united in blood guilt, through our praise and our silence, for the sacrifices to come.

By September, the internal sacrifice was begun in earnest. ''Just about every major economic indicator is now confirming that economic activity fell off a cliff in September,'' said one Wall Street broker, ''and the magnitude of the drop is much larger than anyone anticipated.''[18] The high interest rates produced by the squeezing of the money supply caused a severe drop in sales of cars and homes and an even more severe drop in exports.[19] As consumer demand dried up and capital equipment investment plummeted, output fell, inventories built up and unemployment began its record climb to an official figure of 10.8 percent, a figure con-

Reagan was seen as strangling America.

America watched passively as Reagan carried out the bloody sacrifice.

siderably lower than the reality, if dropouts and the partially employed are counted.

The reaction of the Reagan administration to the disastrous news was to *increase* the pain wherever possible. "The only corrective action the President was considering was further reductions in civilian spending . . . Stockman's OMB has prepared a list of $32 billion in bloody new cuts in everything from food stamps to Head Start programs."[20] The imagery of "bloody cuts" was repeated everywhere in the media. As political columnist Joseph Kraft put it, "There has been blood all over the floor and screaming galore,"[21] an apt image for the human sacrifice which was going on all around him. Yet Kraft, like most of us, managed at the same time to deny the real human sacrifice. His phrase "blood all over the floor and screaming galore" ostensibly referred to government department heads' budget battles, not to live Americans being killed. Reagan, too, managed to acknowledge the bloody sacrifice while at the same time denying it. The problem in America, he told the country in his September 24, 1981 address to the nation, was that we had "hemorrhaged badly and wound up in a sea of red ink." The imagery was quite accurate, both in terms of government borrowing going on (he was having to borrow a record $14 billion a month to keep the government running) and in terms of the number of deaths Reaganomics was causing (over 3,000 a month at that point). But his denial was so effective that when he spoke of hemorrhaging "a sea of red ink" he was actually referring to *previous* administrations, while in fact his program was producing double the deficits and victims of any previous administration.

In demanding that the nation undergo even more "sacrifices" for his "crusade," Reagan consistently voiced our need for human victims while effectively denying our guilt for the sacrifice. One device used by the media in reinforcing this denial was to split the image of the sacrificer from the actual sacrifice. Thus, Reagan would be pictured on one page

of a magazine as holding an ax,
but without a victim. Then, on
the next page, the same ax would
be shown cutting off a victim's
head, but Reagan himself would
be nowhere in sight. In this manner, we could not only save
ourselves the guilt which we
would have otherwise felt if we
had openly portrayed our leader
as a killer of innocent Americans,
but we also could hide the anger
that we felt toward him for being
our hired killer.

For even though we had
delegated to Reagan the job of
chief executioner, we still didn't
like to know he was killing our
neighbors. Since at some level we
knew precisely what he was doing
for us, we also hated him for it,

**We split Reagan's image off from the
actual killings.**

and in several incidents in the fall of 1981 we showed evidence of renewed death wishes toward him. Cartoons showing people wanting

Reagan dead began appearing
for the first time since his
shooting. "Wall Street" was
pictured as wanting him to
"Jump." The "Dems" were
shown carrying him in a coffin
to a cemetery. Yet such open
portrayals of death wishes
were rare, being too little
disguised for comfort. The
death cartoons soon stopped,
and instead a rumor swept
through the Stock Exchange
that Reagan had had a heart
attack.[22] Obviously our death
wishes were not to be denied
an outlet of some sort. We
therefore constructed a new
group-fantasy in order to provide a container for those
death wishes: we imagined

**Death wishes toward Reagan briefly
appeared again.**

that it was the Qaddafi-devil, not us, who wanted to kill Reagan. The CIA, our chief delegate in concocting paranoid threats, produced a list of names and photos of a "Libyan Hit Squad" supposedly hired by Qaddafi to kill Reagan. It did not matter that there was no proof of any such plot. That several of the informants had peddled phoney information previously, that some of those named as part of the "Qaddafi Hit Squad" were actually anti-Qaddafi Amal Shiites, that the "detailed evidence" which Reagan and the CIA promised was never forthcoming and that FBI Director William Webster ended up admitting that no confirmation of any hit squad was ever made and "acknowledged the information may have been planted to make U.S. officials look silly"[23] made little difference to our group-fantasy. The Qaddafi-devil and his "Hit Squad" now contained both our death wishes toward Reagan *and* our death wishes toward our sacrificial victims. The "Hit Squad" *had* to be

Qaddafi was pictured as a scorpion containing our rage and poisoning America.

real, because it contained *an important part of us,* our sadism toward both Reagan and toward our fellow Americans, which, as we saw earlier, had been symbolized as deadly insects (boll weevils and gypsy moths). Qaddafi, too, must therefore be a deadly insect, so he was drawn as a scorpion, ready to poison America. He was a perfect container for all our rage, against Reagan and against our victims. Once again it was our comedians who gave away the motive behind the incident. When a television comedian asked for American donations to a "National Hit Team of Libya,"[24] the audience laughed and cheered wildly. Our death wishes toward Reagan were not very far beneath the surface.

For Reagan personally, the "Libyan Hit Squad" filled the important psychological function of splitting off from awareness all these death wishes. He could label Qaddafi "deranged . . . a mad dog,"[25] order U.S. citizens to leave Libya and for a time rest easy that his paranoid fears about "The Most Dangerous Man in the World," as *Time* called Qaddafi, were isolated far away from our shores. In a world full of tens of thousands of atomic bombs, where a half trillion dollars a year is spent on arms, for the leader of so impotent a country as Libya to be called "The Most Dangerous Man in the World" reveals the growing irrationality of our group-fantasies during this period. The more we proceeded with our internal sacrifice, the more dangerous the world felt to us. Although actual terrorist activities were not increasing at this time,[26]

we began to discuss "the growing international terrorist network" as though there
existed a well-organized army, running
from Russia through Libya to Cuba and
Central America, ready to poison us at
any time. When our cartoonists tried to
picture this "terrorist network," they
drew a very strange-looking figure, bristl-
ing with weapons, spreading across the
globe, looking suspiciously *feminine* for
some reason. To understand this feminine
imagery, one must first look at the infan-
tile source of paranoid imagery in the
political unconscious in somewhat greater
detail.

Qaddafi, the alter ego of
Reagan, was labeled The Most
Dangerous Man in the World.

For most people, the first few years of
life were spent mainly with their mothers,
since it has only been in the past decade
that very many fathers involved
themselves with the daily care of their
young children.[27] When the young child
feels himself or herself to
be bad, it is the mother's
angry look which is most
feared and which
presages the punishment
to come. Therefore, a
period of national
punishment like that of
Reagan's America, when
we imagine we must be
punished for being bad
and having enjoyed
ourselves too much, is
visualized as being
*presided over by disap-
proving eyes*. Sometimes
these eyes are seen as
those of foreign enemies,
but more often they are
pictured as simply
floating above us,
strange, unidentified
staring eyes.

The "world wide terrorist network" was
seen as strangely maternal.

It is this image of persecuting eyes staring at us, demanding punishment, which invariably surfaces during Times of Sacrifice. These

In November 1981, staring eyes burst out everywhere in the media.

paranoid eyes are the same ones as the staring eyes of the wolves in the famous dream of Freud's patient, the Wolf Man, who then broke out in a full-blown paranoid psychosis after the dream.[28] Staring eyes can be found during times of crisis in every country and every age, from the all-powerful "Eye of Horus" of ancient Egypt to the supposedly "hypnotic eyes" of Adolf Hitler which led Germany to its "great sacrifices."[29] The same thing happened during Reagan's Time of Sacrifice. During a two-week period in November of 1981, almost every newsweekly in the nation featured the hypnotic eyes of this imaginary punitive parent who was thought to preside over the nation's sacrificial punishment. The image of the mother's staring eyes was also used by many newspapers when reporting on Sandra O'Conner, who was chosen to be the first woman on the Supreme Court. Her manner, reporters said, was "so stern, her stare so penetrating, that some young lawyers call her 'laser eyes.' "[30] Thus "laser eyes" became the Supreme Judge of our Time of Sacrifice, and we devoted most of our efforts during her confirmation hearings to questioning her attitudes toward "killing babies," i.e., her views on abortion, as though these were all that mattered about her.

If the Supreme Judge of our punishment was often symbolically seen as a stern mother, those punished were usually symbolically seen as children, in accordance with the basic family drama in our unconscious. This could be seen in the choice of political symbols, as when the victims of budget cuts were often portrayed as children or as when the government was shown as killing rather than protecting innocent young animals—Bambi's head being displayed mounted on the office wall of Secretary of Interior James Watt, who was supposedly hired to protect baby deer. Even when a general symbol for the economic sacrifice had to be portrayed, more often than not the victims

The government was seen as killing instead of protecting the young.

were drawn as tiny little figures, as though they were symbolic babies.

But here again the media metaphor was also carried out in reality, in the deaths of real children. When cuts were proposed by Reagan in Social Security payments to the elderly, the national outcry was so great that he was forced to back down. But when cuts were proposed for Aid to Families with Dependent Children, school lunches, child care food programs, food stamps, child abuse programs and dozens of other government activities directly affecting the welfare and lives of children, few spoke up, and those few who did were puzzled by the impotence of their cries. It was not just that, as one commentator put it, "kids have no con-

Those sacrificed were often seen as small as children.

stituency to protest; battered babies don't vote.''[31] Parents vote, and if hurting and killing children had not been essential to our Time of Sacrifice, the outcry of parents would easily have stopped the slaughter of the innocents as quickly as it had stopped the proposed cutback of Social Security checks.

Yet article after article was written during the winter of 1981-2 on the rise in infant mortality in areas hardest hit by budget cutbacks and unemployment, on the over one million additional children on the poverty rolls, on the six million children who had lost health coverage because of layoffs of their parents, of the half million children who had lost health services because of the closing by the government of 239 community health centers, of the hundreds of additional children who would be battered to death because of Reagan's cutback of almost all of the funds for the highly successful National Center on Child Abuse and Neglect—in all, over twenty million children suffering needless pain, hunger and death with barely a mourner in sight.[32] During those cold winter nights, we all watched television and saw nightly scenes of children sleeping in the snow under bridges because their parents had been laid off and scenes of newborn infants dying on camera because of lack of funding to the government's program of diet supplement for poor pregnant and nursing women. Yet we never really felt *guilty* for the dead and suffering children who passed before our eyes. ''The Reagan safety net is a myth,'' reported television commentator Bill Moyers. ''People are dying as the result of these cuts.''[33] Yet we felt nothing. Nor did Reagan. When attacked by Rep. Bolling for having caused ''human suffering,'' he retorted: ''Look, my program hasn't resulted in anyone getting thrown out in the snow or dying.''[34] Denial was total. What had happened to the guilt?

The usual answer to this question is that we avoided guilt through use of various rationalizations, by saying it was someone else's fault, not ours, by blaming everything on ''the impersonal forces of the economic system'' and so on. Yet rationalizations as transparent as these would not by themselves have been enough to still our conscience when incidents happened which arose to expose them.

As one instance, during the Christmas week at the end of 1981, the government, to show that Reagan was a caring president, released 30 million pounds of cheese to be given to the hungry Americans whom they had previously said did not exist. As millions of people lined up for their five-pound blocks of cheese, it was uncomfortably obvious to all that the government had the means to alleviate hunger during the recession by giving away much of the 2.4 billion pounds of surplus milk, cheese and butter which it had bought and was storing to hold up dairy prices. In fact, the government could give away this food at a cost that turned out to be *less* than the $1 million a day it cost to store it. With the gigantic stockpile being added to at the rate of $6 million a day, it was obvious that handing out only a tiny portion of our huge growing stockpile of dairy products—a stockpile which grew by two-thirds during the recession years—while warehousing the rest at a higher cost and letting it eventually rot meant we *wanted* people to be hungry. It was as transparent an act of cruelty as President Roosevelt's order to plough baby pigs into the ground during the Great Depression (again, to hold up farmers' prices) rather than giving them to hungry Americans to eat. When one Congressman complained that he could not understand "why food was withheld and destroyed even as people went hungry," another, who voted to cut back on the distribution, replied that having to deliberately cause people to go hungry was "perhaps the greatest paradox that we face in our country today."[35] Since such moments of clarity of motive so often revealed the transparency of our economic rationalizations, the question remains: what happens to our guilt? Why do we almost *never* feel any guilt for the death of innocent people we hurt and kill through political means?

The answer to this question is that *we displace our guilt into criminals.* Every period in history when we increase our sacrificial victims through economic means also shows a parallel increase in our efforts to punish criminals. Reagan's Time of Sacrifice was no exception. Even though overall homicide rates were not increasing during 1981,[36] Reagan and the media invented a "crime epidemic" which was purported to be sweeping the country. Reagan himself led the nation in this group-fantasy. In the same speeches in which he asked for "more sacrifices" by the American people, he also decried the new "American crime epidemic" whereby criminals are "quite literally getting away with murder."[37] Language such as this is the only evidence that Reagan ever dimly recognized that he himself was "quite literally getting away with murder" in his economic program. Combined with his claim that "no one was dying" from Reaganomics, his insistent repetition that "the people of the community are really suffering" from a crime wave reveals the shift of guilt from himself—and ourselves—to criminals.

If Reagan needed criminals into whom he could dump his own guilt, it makes sense that at the same time as he was demanding a "war on crime" he actually was cutting law enforcement funds. For if crime were really to be reduced, his guilt would then return back to him. So law enforcement funds had to be reduced to keep crime high. Only such irrational motives can explain the public's attitude toward crime, an attitude which includes an addiction toward and fascination with criminals that betrays deeply irrational group-fantasy sources. Since punishment of criminals is the goal of our laws, not reduction of crime, studies are easily ignored which show that therapy and guidance are far more effective and less costly than punishment and incarceration. For instance, during Reagan's term some states considered new laws mandating ten-year jail terms for people who kill or maim others while driving when drunk. Yet it would have been impossible to get any attention for a proposal to give intensive therapy and guidance to the same people, even though the cost would be a fraction of the $100,000 per year per person cost of jail cells and the results far more effective than punishment by incarceration in assuring that offenders would not drive while drunk in the future. Yet rather than do something which might actually reduce crime, we in Reagan's America spent most of our time on such emotional issues as the restoration of capital punishment, in order to accomplish our aim of punishing "the criminal in ourselves."

The more children Reagan sacrificed, the more local newspapers discovered such group-fantasies as "an epidemic of child abuse sweeping the city."[38] As the official jobless rate moved past the 9 percent rate early in 1982, Wall Street exhulted in the new docility of workers. "We are thrilled," said Peter Grace, chairman of W. R. Grace & Co. "We've finally turned the country around."[39] "I'm really excited," said W. J. Sanders, III, chairman of Micro Devices, Inc. "We are unshackling the real talent of this country and exposing the inept."[40] Some of

Reagan was shown pushing the victims of The Time of Sacrifice over the sacrificial cliff.

these "inept" included the disabled, an early Reagan target even though the Social Security disability fund which supported them had plenty of money in it from workers' disability contributions.[41] Over 500,000 disability cases were reviewed in Reagan's first year, and an astounding 45 percent were terminated on flimsy pretexts, "even though both their doctors and the Social Security Administration's own physicians agree that the individuals cannot perform even ordinary day-to-day functions of living," according to the *Los Angeles Times* report on the crackdown.[42] Equally as "inept" were black youths, whose unemployment rate topped 50 percent, several million people who had grown too discouraged to look for work, additional millions who ran out of unemployment benefits—so that, in Detroit, many unemployed purposely drank heavily or took drugs so they could enter alcoholic and drug wards which by law had to house and feed them—and many other helpless or powerless people, all symbolically "inept" children to be punished.

Not included as "inept" were the wealthy, who alone benefited from the three-quarter trillion dollars in tax cuts (over the first five years), the largest tax giveaway in the history of any country, "likely to go down in history as the single most irresponsible fiscal action in modern times," according to former Budget Director James Schlesinger.[43] The result was a predictible record rise in executive salaries (up 12 percent in recession 1981), a rise in sales of Rolls-Royce, Cadillac and Mercedes cars, a boom in expensive home swimming pools and record purchase prices for Manhatten co-ops, mostly for cash.[44] "We've found that the very wealthy are spending more money than normal," wrote *Newsweek*, deadpan. *U.S. News* put it more bluntly on their cover: "FLAUNTING WEALTH: IT'S BACK IN STYLE."[45] As Stockman had put it, "The hogs were really feeding. The greed level, the level of opportunism, just got out of control."[46]

Yet this was precisely what we wanted to accomplish, to feed the top while punishing the bottom. Otherwise, there would have been at least a token fight by the Democrats against Reaganomics. Instead, as one commentator put it, "In Washington people remarked on the magical disappearance of the Democratic Party."[47] Initially, Democratic leaders pretended that their acquiesence was only tactical. "Democrats Have a Plan: Sit Back, Relax, Enjoy," headlined *The New York Times*, citing a "beaming" Speaker of the House Tip O'Neill, Jr. as saying "I think I'll sit on the sidelines a while."[48]

Yet he would sit forever if he thought all the pain would turn the country against Reagan. Everyone agreed that Reagan's image was *enhanced* by his sacrificial actions, not tarnished. Puzzled, most commentators ascribed this not to the efficacy of sacrifice but to some mysterious quality in Reagan's personality. "It doesn't much matter what happens," said

New York magazine. "The people like Ronald Reagan."[49] "For the first time in years, Washington has a president it really likes, one who clearly relishes the role and is good at it to boot," echoed *The Washington Post*'s Haynes Johnson.[50] "The president is still riding high in the polls," said another reporter, "because in the domestic area Reagan has *acted*."[51] "Just about everybody here thinks Reagan can walk on water," conceded a Republican politician in Indiana.[52] A Democrat in Houston who had voted for Reagan thought his decisiveness was more important than anything else; sounding like a woman in love with a man who beats her up, she told reporters, "He'll either make us or break us. He is a leader and I got tired of not having a leader."[53] As another woman from North Carolina told *The Washington Post*, even if everyone were worse off because of the recession, she herself felt "better off mentally."[54]

The media during this period were filled with praise for the beneficial effects of the punishment. "IN PRAISE OF RECESSION," hymned William Safire in *The New York Times*, adding, "we must not quit when we are winning."[55] If anything, most political commentators considered Reagan *not cruel enough* for the task we gave him to do for us. "He may be too nice to be president," said the nation's foremost expert on the subject, Richard Nixon.[56] Haynes Johnson agreed: "One word springs forward to describe him. Nice."[54] Those few who disagreed were labeled Reds. "They clearly are militant radicals," TV announcer Gabe Pressman pronounced as he watched 10,000 very middle-class demonstrators in New York protest the presentation of the humanitarian award to Reagan for "courageous leadership in humanitarian affairs."[58] Nothing, no note of criticism, no hint of guilt, must be allowed to deter us from cleansing our nation in our mystical sacrificial rebirth.

After Reagan moved into his third, or "collapse," phase, overt birth images began to appear in the media.

We moved into a "collapse" phase.

Reaganonomics was pictured as a giant egg, with Reagan praying for the birth to take place soon. The more the recession deepened, the more pain and death inflicted on the sacrificial victims, the more miraculous the rebirth of America would be. "We are on the verge of a recovery like nothing ever seen in this country," said the Under Secretary of Treasury.[59] *Business Week* agreed, shouting from its front cover "HERE COMES THE RECOVERY!" Many Americans even

Reagan prayed for our rebirth via Reaganomics.

imagined their wishes had come true and Reagan had already accomplished the rebirth. For instance, although the government was borrowing a record $16 billion a month just to meet its bills, pollsters were startled to find two out of every five Americans thought Reagan had in fact already balanced the budget as he had promised.[60] As Reagan himself put it, "There's a spiritual revival going on in this country." Like all revivalist movements, it was aimed at a rebirth through the purging of our sinful excesses. Those who were puzzled by the "triumph of faith over evidence,"[61] as economist Lester Thurow called the fantasies that Reaganomics was working, didn't understand how much Reagan's America was essentially a *religious* movement designed to produce an "America Reborn" through sacrifice.

Of course, sometimes reality intruded. Then Reagan and his associates would blame business or Wall Street for not producing the miraculous rebirth. "We gave them more than they ever dreamed," complained the Republican minority leader, Rep. Robert Michel, "and you'd think there would be more of a quid pro quo." "We have carried through our commitments," agreed Secretary of the Treasury Donald Regan. "But where is the business response? Where are the new research and development initiatives? Where are the new plants? Where are the expansion plans?"[62] That business had no conceivable motive to expand production when demand had dried up and industrial utilization had been reduced to 67 percent seemed to escape these economic experts. They really *believed* in the miracles produced by pain. "Reaganomists: Forge Ahead Despite Pain," headlined *The Miami Herald*.[63] In a revealing "Freudian slip," Reagan told a fund-raising dinner, "Now we are trying to get unemployment to go up, and I think we're going to succeed." Senator Pressler agreed: "It would not be a good idea to saw him off at the legs at this point."[64]

A baby boom was imagined.

During the spring of 1982, images of the rebirth group-fantasy multiplied in the media, until they subliminally dominated the feeling-tone of every American's daily life, though they were not consciously noticed by most people. A "new baby boom" was proclaimed, although the actual birth rate per potential mother was dropping.[65] Pictures of pregnant women were displayed on the front covers of magazines to show what was happening. In fact, *everything* suddenly seemed to be pregnant that spring, from Reaganomics to the atomic bomb. Phrases associated with birth feelings began to be used with increasing frequency, such as "It's like waiting for a baby to be born"[66] or "the pressure was building from all sides"[67] or "This Administration believes that life begins at conception and ends at birth."[68] Discussions of abortion multiplied. Reagan even personally endorsed a bizarre plan by anti-abortion advocates in California to hold a fetus funeral for 17,000 aborted fetuses which the group had collected.[69]

New legislation also seemed to be stuck in the birth canal that spring. *The Washington Post* cartoonist drew Reagan as though he were helping Tip O'Neill give birth, and the caption right next to the cartoon quoted Reagan as saying, "You may make me crap a pineapple, but you can't make me crap a cactus," as though Reagan himself were the one who felt he was giving birth.[70]

Everything seemed to be pregnant in the spring of 1982.

As Reagan told the nation, America would "soon emerge from this dark tunnel of recession"—the same dark tunnel which America had hoped to see "the light at the end of" during the Vietnam war. Everything seemed to be going down that dark birth tunnel that spring: the White House, the economy, all of Washington, Reagan himself, the American people. The world was felt to be one giant hole, and we were

We all felt as if we were going down a dark birth tunnel.

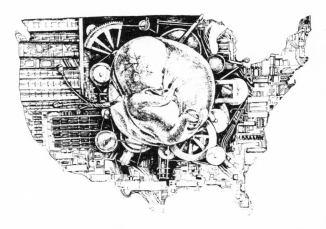

Reindustrialization was seen as a fetus in the womb.

dropping into it, as we felt we did long ago during our own births.[71]

Reagan announced in April that we were "approaching a climactic stage," one in which he began to hear "a drum beat"—ostensibly of criticism, but equally the loud heart beat of the mother in labor. American revitalization and reindustrialization were imagined to be the prize at the end of the rebirth tunnel, and were pictured as a fetus in the womb awaiting birth. Uncle Sam, too, was pictured as standing in the watery womb,

We felt like we were in the womb, awaiting birth.

looking at a drawing of where we were—in the womb-like belly of a whale, ready to begin our birth travail. It would be terribly painful, but it was unavoidable, and the sooner we got it over with the better.

With birth beginning, with the pressures building, it seemed as if "Mother Nature" was "going berserk," as a *U.S. News* cover put it. With our faith in the economy collapsing, as our mother's womb once did, we imagined birth would feel as if the world were ending, as it felt during our own births, when the contraction pressures and hypoxia (lack of oxygen) made us feel as if we were dying. Therefore, newspapers across the country began running articles describing fears of "The End of the World," supposedly in connection with the chance lining up of the planets which took place that spring, in about the same manner as the previous year, when no notice had been taken of it.[72]

Jumpin' Jupiter! The End of the World!

We feared birth would feel like the end of the world.

In fact, our apocalyptic fantasies soon reached such a degree of reality to us that we became newly concerned with the possibility of a nuclear holocaust ending the world. Observers were puzzled at the timing of the new concern over nuclear war. "Why," asked *The New York Times*, "37 years into the Atomic Age, the sudden rush of concern? Has last year's European peace movement crossed the Atlantic? Is it that a new generation has grown up ignorant of Strangelove? Have older generations failed fully to appreciate the risks?"[73] Unless one recognized the birth fantasy, the sudden and all-too-temporary attention to atomic apocalypse—climaxing in the massive Freeze rally in New York City on June 12th—was inexplicable.

As did Carter's America during its "collapse" phase, Reagan's America seemed everywhere to be full of falling and collapsing feelings, which could only be cleansed through some apocalyptic upheaval, some acting out in reality of the powerful fantasies we shared.

Our apocalyptic fantasies included a renewed interest in nuclear war.

We seemed to be going off a birth cliff.

We were trapped, unable to be born.

We felt stuck in the birth canal.

Yet nothing in reality seemed to be available to us which we could use to move the birth fantasy along. No foreign nations threatened, and none seemed to be forthcoming in the near future to accept our challenge and deflect our bad feelings outward. Everything seemed to make us feel trapped in this unborn position. Our economy was still falling. No miraculous rebirth could be found there soon. We were unprepared emotionally to go to war. All seemed increasingly hopeless. Just as the baby feels its birth pains are endless, we, too, felt closed in, without hope, unable to get a breath of relief, stuck in the birth canal forever.

This imagery of being stuck in the birth canal dominated the country's cartoons that April, and the political language reflected the fantasy. "Treasury Secretary Donald T. Regan pronounced the national economy 'dead in the water' yesterday," the newspapers reported.[74] We were in fact "in a deep trough," the White House press secretary confirmed soon after.[75] It seemed as if we might lie in the womb, "dead in the water," forever. How could the birth be pushed along? Where could we look for help?

The answer to our dilemma came from events even then moving to a climax in the South Atlantic.

"Don't just stand there crying 'It's dead in the water . . . It's dead in the water.' Gimme a hand!"

We felt "dead in the water."

6

TRIAL WARS
"What a Cute Little War"

Like Ronald Reagan, British Prime Minister Margaret Thatcher had been elected to produce a "rebirth of spirit" through an internal sacrifice (recession) and an external sacrifice (war).

By the beginning of 1982, she had succeded in her first task of reducing the prosperity of the Sixties and Seventies by almost doubling the British unemployment rate during her first three years in office. Yet the threat which prosperity posed for the near-Victorian consciences of most Englishmen had not been permanently removed, despite Tory pledges of "austerity." Sparked by increasing North Sea oil income and by the economic productivity of a vigorous new psychoclass, British economic indicators, including gross domestic product, had begun turning up after the summer of 1981, producing fresh anxiety which would somehow have to be purged.

Mrs. Thatcher was personally blamed for the malaise produced by the economic upturn. The Tories dropped to only 30 percent approval in the polls, and Thatcher was well into the "collapse" phase of her term by the beginning of 1982. Something would have to be done soon to deflect the anger from her to an appropriate "enemy," who would then have to be convinced it must cooperate in a blood sacrifice that would, in fantasy, drain off the "bad blood"—the guilty conscience, the rage—which was increasingly felt to be polluting England. As one observer put it, "Maggie Thatcher needs blood for her constituency..."[1]

Like America, England was too civilized to start a war openly for sacrificial purposes. A developed nation usually begins a war by sending hidden messages to another country which has poor impulse control, messages suggesting that a war would now be desirable, and then sitting back and waiting for the more impulse-prone nation to help it act out its unconscious wishes. The process is identical to the way parents often give their children hidden commands to act out the parents' secret wishes and then punish the children for being "bad."

Most modern nations keep several impulsive "children" around to be able to use when they need a blood sacrifice. England kept her dispute with Argentina over the Falkland Islands alive for decades for just this purpose, since a simple "leaseback" compromise had been worked out some time before which negotiators admitted made the problem one which "would take ten minutes to solve if both sides were willing."[2] Through a series of hidden messages suggesting that they were emotionally abandoning the islands—actions ranging from the denial of British citizenship to the Falklanders to the abrupt removal of the British ship *Endurance*[3]—Argentina was unconsciously invited to occupy the tiny islands, while being led to believe that England would take no military steps to oppose the occupation.

The bait was an attractive one to Argentina. This was not because the islands had any real value to her, but because she herself was also in a "collapse" group-fantasy of such explosive proportions—including record unemployment and inflation—that *La Prensa* had to admit a month before the invasion that "the only thing which can save this government is a war."[4]

Britain, however, was not the only nation encouraging Argentina to solve her internal emotional problems by military force. America had been telling Argentina's General Galtieri to become more aggressive militarily ever since Reagan took office. Galtieri, like Reagan's father, was an impulse-prone alcoholic, and Reagan knew how easy it was to provoke him to violence. America poured military supplies and training into Argentina's small army in return for Argentina's sending troops to Honduras for our "covert" war against Nicaragua and for promising help in a secret Reagan plan to blockade Cuba.[5] Although America did not publicly suggest an invasion of the Falklands, many of Reagan's people openly encouraged Galtieri's military impulsiveness.   U.N. ambassador Jeane Kirkpatrick told startled British diplomats the night of Galtieri's invasion that it was "not armed aggression" because Argentina already owned the islands.[6] Similarly, Alexander Haig had so openly encouraged Argentina's military adventurousness that her Foreign Minister, Nicanor Costa Mendes, bluntly told Haig, "If there's a war, it's all your fault." America, too, was using Argentina as its "impulsive child." When we later condemned the invasion, Argentina felt shocked and betrayed.[8]

The reaction of both sides to the invasion was openly jingoistic and filled with slogans stressing the need for "national sacrifice." The British task force was sent off to the islands accompanied by the cheers of Parliament shouting "action not words" and jubulant crowds weeping for joy in the Plaza de Mayo. "Like two schoolboys itching for a fight," said one observer, "they'll not be satisfied until there's some blood on the floor."[9]

American excitement over the war was almost as manic as that of Britain. "Bravo Britain," one American newsman shouted. "Bash them!"[10] England had shown us how to relieve our group-fantasy dilemma. They, like us, were stuck in the "collapse" phase, unable to be reborn through the sacrifice of their unemployed. They, like us, were becoming filled with rage, along with fears that their leader was impotent to help them control their emotions. "The world is watching today to see what the Brits will

America became excited over the war and displayed an erect phallus and two testicles.

do," said American columnist Patrick Buchanan. "And the world will be a worse place if the Brits do not put up a fight...As Maggie Thatcher must realize, if Great Britain accepts this humiliation, Great Britain is finished."[11] The Brits seemed to know how to do these things better than the Americans: you set up your kid to humiliate you, then you "bash 'em." It worked in the family, and it worked in wars.

Some Americans even fantasied that we could join Great Britain in her sacrifice. Why couldn't *we* also have our "Glorious Little War" now? "Some U.S. ships sailing south would concentrate the junta's mind on the fact that the U.S. intends to guarantee the success of its NATO ally," suggested *Newsweek*'s George F. Will. The fantasy of England, America and Argentina all shedding blood together on one tiny island might seem odd, but it fits the fact that both Britain and America were shipping sophisticated weapons to

We felt that only a war could complete our rebirth.

Holding a sacrifice on a small island was felt to be cute.

Argentina right up to the invasion, pumping both deadly feelings and deadly weapons into the same impulsive delegate. So confused, in fact, were all three countries in American minds that when ABC-TV commentator Carl Bernstein compared the Falklands battle to "the Battle of Yorktown" it seemed logical somehow.[13] Part of *us* was sailing south with the British fleet—our sacrificial wishes. We had had to sit passively and watch *Star Wars* movies for too long. Why couldn't we be like the British and fight, not wait? "When Iran's militants seized our embassy in Tehran and took our subjects hostage...we might have responded as Prime Minister Margaret Thatcher responded, by assembling an armada and mounting an invasion," wrote columnist James Kilpatrick,[14] sending a message to the President.

Sexual fantasies were put into the war zone.

But it is not just beginning a war which requires a macho display of tumescent manhood. All aspects of war have hidden sexual content, and much of war's excitement for both citizen and soldier is patently sexual. The British tabloids captured their sexual fantasies accurately as the fleet headed south: "STICK IT UP YOUR JUNTA"; "THE TIME FOR TALK IS OVER: OUR LADS WANT TO ZAP THEM"; "A PUNCH UP YOUR JUNTA", and so on. War begins with a group-fantasy of rape because it is our own unconscious sexual fantasies which are put into the "enemy." Just as the internal sacrifice of recession requires a two-step fantasy of seeing the unemployed as (1) containing our greedy wishes and (2) being punished for those wishes, so, too, the external sacrifice of war requires us to see both our own "lads" and "the enemy" as (1) containing our sexual and aggressive wishes and (2) being punished for those wishes.

Like all sacrifices, wars are combats with our own id, whereby we first act out and then punish our desires in the person of those killed. The youngest and sexiest are chosen as victims, just as in many primitive cultures it is the most handsome warrior who is sacrificed, right after having ritual sex. The group-fantasy is that their blood, their vitality, drains off our dangerous pleasures, our sexuality, into the ground.

Time described this basic fantasy well, just before we sent our first troops into Vietnam. In January 1964, in a special issue on "SEX IN THE U.S.," *Time* saw a dangerous "demise of Puritanism" in America due to "Freudian psychology," and imagined that

> America is one big Orgone Box...From innumerable screens and stages, posters and pages, it flashes the larger-than-life-sized images of sex from countless racks and shelves, it pushes the books which a few years ago were considered pornography [with] the message that sex will save you and libido make you free.[15]

The group-fantasy solution to this dangerous buildup of sexuality was that it could only be controlled by shifting it over to Vietnam. The fantasy could best be seen in the words of President Johnson, who saw Vietnam as a *whore* with whom he was having an affair:

> I left the woman I really loved—the Great Society—in order to get involved with that bitch of a war on the other side of the world...[16]

War is a "bitch." You have to give her a "punch up her junta," and then you have to kill her to wipe out your shameful sexual desires.

This is why wars are initially always a return of the repressed id, containing both heterosexual rape fantasies and homosexual fantasies, such as when Johnson said of his bombing of Vietnam, "I didn't just screw Ho Chi Minh; I cut his pecker off," or, "When I call a bombing halt...then Ho Chi Minh shoves his trucks right up my ass."[17] That going to war involves sexual excitement is not only made obvious by the use of such language as "carrying a Big Stick," "displays of firmness" and "the stiffening of our national will" but also in the feelings of the average soldier when he is being honest about how combat feels. Here, for instance, is how one American soldier in Vietnam described his feelings about being in combat:

It's absolutely the most intense continual excitement I've ever known in my life. I'm not sure how to describe the energy you feel...the excitement was there for everybody. You were using that finger to try to take somebody's life, and that sends a real charge through you.[18]

Yet it is finally the superego, not the id—the punishment, not the sex—that wins out in every war. Occasionally this can be seen in the language that is used to conduct the war—as, for instance, when Secretary of State Dean Rusk said the reason why America built up its troops so slowly in Vietnam was to prevent Hanoi and Moscow from having "an orgasm of decision-making" which a fast buildup might produce.[19] Usually, however, our need to punish the containers of our hidden desires is too well defended to be revealed so openly. It easily gets buried beneath our rage at the "enemy" and our grief over the death of the "boys who have sacrificed so much for their countries." Yet it remains our own sexuality—and, by extension, our vitality, our best hopes, our "life blood"—which is sacrificed through all those dead bodies, and our own sexuality and vitality which is mourned as the coffins return.

It was sometimes even possible to find the hidden sexual content in Reagan's speeches on international politics. Just as earlier he saw "sexual orgies and communism" linked at Berkeley, so, too, as President he imagined that

The Soviet Union underlies all the unrest that is going on. If they weren't engaged in this game of dominoes, there wouldn't be any hot spots in the world.

Although the term "hot spots" is sometimes used as a synonym for "trouble spots," during Reagan's formative years in the Midwest it had a more frequent meaning: "hot spots" were *sexy places*, such as nightclubs or brothels, where one goes for some "action." Similarly, the use of the "domino" metaphor is an image right out of childhood, for though Russians don't play dominoes, most Americans did in their childhood. So when Reagan says that the Russians are having all the fun, playing dominoes and getting into all the "hot spots," he is using the Russians as containers for his own repressed id wishes. And then when he asks Americans to join him in a crusade to wipe out these "Russian hot spots," he is using the language of his puritanical mother, who taught him always to control his emotions and never, never give in to them lest he become like his alcoholic father.

When the Falklands became a "hot spot," therefore, America, too, became sexually excited. Our papers ran pictures of the British woman who had just "stripped off her blouse and bra to thunderous applause" and threw them to the troops aboard ship, under the headline "FALKLANDS OR BUST!"[20] The media made the war seem like a lot of fun. American columnists vied with each other over who

War was seen as more exciting than diplomacy.

could make up the funniest jokes about the sheep that would be killed in the invasion: "It's a lead-pipe cinch a couple of sheep are going to be run over before the day is out. That's where the feature writers move in for interviews with the weeping sheep owner," said Russel Baker in the *New York Times.*[21]

When the thousand men who were indeed sacrificed like sheep began coming home in bags, the American press, like the British, was filled with the language of national rebirth, "the Falklands spirit," evidence of "a renewed national pride and self-confidence."[22] It felt *good* for us to have a cleansing war around again, even if it cleansed only by proxy. Reagan's first address to the nation after the Falklands war began opened with fantasy language startlingly different than the usual "collapse" language of his previous five speeches:

Fantasy Analysis of
Opening Words of Reagan's Address to Nation
May 10, 1982

Fantasy Words	*Interpretation*
pleasure...warm...clean out ...guilt...happy...eat... heart...life...renew	What a pleasure, how warm it feels, to have a war clean out our guilt. We are happy to eat the heart full of life to renew us.

The imagery was identical to that of the Aztec sacrificial ritual, where the old polluted heart was "cleaned out" and the new heart, "full of life," was eaten to "renew" the nation.

"THAT FALKLANDS FIGHTING DIDN'T EXACTLY DO THATCHER ANY HARM"

We learned a lesson from "the Falklands spirit."

All we saw in America was the group-fantasy lesson. No American paper mentioned the thousand dead, nor the large areas of the islands which were now closed to human use, nor the several billions of dollars the war and its aftermath cost (tens of millions of dollars per Falklands householder). No American blurted out, as Denis Healey did in England, that Mrs. Thatcher was "glorying in slaughter." All that we took from the carnage was the lesson of "the Falklands spirit" —that it felt *good* to sacrifice "the lads." Mrs. Thatcher's polls soared, and she would soon be re-elected by a landslide. Why not here, too? Would we not be as grateful to Ronald Reagan if he would sacrifice "our lads" in a war we could win? He had not promised us in his election campaign not to send our boys into battle. What he had promised was that "never again will we send our boys to fight and die *in a war we do not intend to win.*" Couldn't we, too, find a little country we could be assured of overpowering so we, too, could get our sexual thrill and then bury our sexuality with the dead? Would we not be grateful, too, and reward our leader with a landslide re-election?

When Reagan went to England and addressed Parliament right after Falklands, he thanked the British people for their wonderful example to America, for having shown us how in war "the forces of good ultimately rally and triumph over evil...Let us be shy no longer," he proposed. "Let us go to our strength." The British had shown us, according to Reagan, how "a great victory in war [could] leave Marxism-Leninism on the ash heap of history." If we followed their example, we, too, could complete

Cartoonists began depicting Reagan as a bird of prey after Falklands.

our rebirth and clean out our polluted nation.

Beginning with the summer of 1982, after Reagan had said we should "be shy no longer" and "go to our strength," cartoonists began regularly portraying Reagan as a regal bird of prey—an eagle or a vulture—and the White House as a phallic weapon, reflecting our growing preoccupation with war. At the same time, since cartoons, like dreams, contain wishes, these were messages to Reagan that we *wanted* a cleansing war, to complete our rebirth, to control our sexuality and to end the threat posed by our dangerous "permissive society." Headlines like "Mideast Nightmare: Search for a Way Out" were paired with others saying "End of the Permissive Society" to make clear this link between our search for war and the end of sexual permissiveness.

The White House turned into a phallic weapon in our fantasies.

When Israel invaded Lebanon in June 1982, American reaction was identical to what it was to the Falklands war. Israel, like Argentina, had been encouraged to be one of America's "impulsive children" for some time. Earlier in the year, Reagan had "winked"[24] at the bombing of Baghdad by Israel, and then secretly had given his agreement to Defense Minister Ariel Sharon that a "small" invasion into Lebanon would not be opposed.[25] In fact, it was an open secret among Washington reporters that Secretary of State Alexander Haig was backing an Israeli invasion of Lebanon and that the U.S. army had been promised that samples of Russian tanks and equipment captured in Lebanon would be sent to America.[26]

The "nightmare" of war was felt to give us "a way out" from our "permissive society."[23]

Israeli group-fantasies also were well into their "collapse" stage at this time. Begin, using the "cleansing" and "purifying" language of external sacrifice, ordered his troops across the quiet Lebanon border, splitting all hatred off from himself into the enemy and sending his faltering polls soaring. American cartoonists reflected accurately the group-fantasy being played out on the international stage. Begin was shown as firing a

Begin was felt to be shooting Reagan's phallus.

America wished for wars without end.

phallic cannon, complete with two testicles...but the cannon seemed to be growing out of *Reagan's* groin. Israel and America seemed fused in our minds. "Israel had again done the West a favor," said one observer,[27] accurately reflecting our delegation of wishes. Haig was so pleased at the invasion that he slipped when telling reporters that Israel had had only small losses, saying that "we" had had only small losses, another example of the fusion in our minds of our two countries.[28] Columnists commented on "Reagan's refusal to utter a word of criticism of Israel's bloody romp through Lebanon,"[29] and wrote columns like the one by Mary McGrory in the *Washington Post* headlined "REAGAN IS MELLOW ABOUT SLAUGHTER IN LEBANON."[30]

American polls showed rising support for the Israelis during the invasion,[31] and Begin was so grateful for Reagan's support that he called him the "best president for Israel since Richard Nixon."[32] Israeli impulsiveness, termed "an example of spirit for America to follow" by columnist Max Lerner,[33] taught us the same group-fantasy lesson as Falklands—thousands of dead victims would be needed to cleanse us of our pollution, as the Israelis had been cleansed of theirs.

Ronald Reagan and the American people both agreed that war was the only way out. The unconscious emotional decision to go to war was made that summer. Reagan's June 30, 1982 press conference announced to everyone watching on television that we, too, would soon go to war to relieve our feelings of being stuck "dead in the water," but that we would have to wait a while until he, Reagan, gave us the "green light."

Fantasy Analysis of
Presidential News Conference
June 30, 1982

Fantasy Words	*Interpretation*
President: cruelly...cut...cut... cut...cut...hit... cut...mess...hope... hurting...strengthen	We must cruelly cut and hit someone to clean up the mess. I hope to end your hurting and strengthen the nation.
Question: cut off arms? slaughter? killing?	Will we have to cut off arms, slaughter and begin killing?
President: bloodshed...terror ...sorrow...hot spots ...tragedy...keeping the lid on...blood- shed...dead in the water	Bloodshed, terror and sorrow will be needed to drain the hot spots and prevent a tragedy. We have been keeping the lid on so far, but bloodshed is needed to stop feeling dead in the water.
Question: attack? fight?	Will we attack and fight?
President: Yes...hurt...hurt... dumped...relieves... day of reckoning	Yes, our hurt can be dumped into others. It relieves us when the day of reckoning comes.
Question: green light?	Is this the green light?
President:green light...sur- prise...starvation	The green light will be a sur- prise. Until then, it will feel like starvation.
Question: blind? dangling?	Until then we'll be blind? You'll keep us dangling?
President: blind	Yes, you'll be blind.
Question: bombs? war?	Then bombs and war?
President: bomb...attack	Yes, then a bomb attack.

From the summer of 1982 on, the group-fantasies of most of America slowly regressed into a full-blown paranoid delusion. Psychotic ways of thinking became more and more prevalent in the conduct of government, exactly in the same manner as an individual who develops a paranoid delusion. Psychoanalyst John Frosch describes the typical stages of a paranoid delusion in his book *The Psychotic Process*:

A man becomes increasingly concerned about some bodily function. He goes from doctor to doctor and has all sorts of tests. Temporarily he is reassured by the negative findings. Eventually, however, he returns to the same symptoms and complaints, or variations thereof. Little by little his bodily functioning becomes his main preoccupation, in a sense his whole life and whole concern. If the patient remains at this stage, his clinical condition is characterized as hypochondriasis.

But further developments may ensue. The patient may become extremely worried about his drowsiness, his headaches, the way his stomach feels, etc. Suddenly one day, in a flash, it becomes clear to him when all this began. It was the day his neighbor offered him a cup of coffee. Now that he thinks back, he remembers that it really did taste kind of funny and as soon as he drank it he did notice a slight dizziness and confusion. The coffee was poisoned; it affected his brain, his stomach, and other parts of his body. They have begun to disintegrate and deteriorate. Here we see the emergence of somatic delusions. With this retrospective falsification of the origins of his physical complaints, a familiar mechanism comes into play—projection. The patient's somatic sensations, the peculiar way he feels, are attributed to external forces; they are something that someone caused to happen to him.

It is with this sudden realization—"Now I understand it"—that we see the beginning development of the systematized delusion. Yet this burst of clarification brings in its wake a shift of anxiety, and the confusional state may subside. It is not beside the point that sometimes the initiation of a delusional system brings a kind of reintegration of the personality in other areas. Systematized delusions are sometimes considered to have an integrative effect on the ego.

The process may stop here. But let us see what happens if the condition progresses. The plot thickens. Groups of people are involved. The patient is the focus of a conspiracy, involving at first a few, then more people (both close to him and not). It may grow into a worldwide conspiracy. These people are out to get him, to hurt him, to stop some important function he has to perform. But why pick on him? Why has he been made the focus of a worldwide conspiracy? Obviously he must be an important person. Now we begin to see the beginning evolution of the delusion into the grandiose stage. The patient's own importance expands. Why are so many people involved? Little by little, the idea takes shape that this is all an attempt to interfere with an important mission entrusted to him. He is to save the world. He begins to see himself as the messenger of God, or even God Himself.[34]

Like the individual who goes through a paranoid episode, Reagan's America would go through the same stages during the following years, as more and more of reality would come to be dominated by internal delusions. We had just spent several months worrying about staring eyes and being stuck in a birth canal, "dead in the water." We would now spend the next several months feeling we were being poisoned, by Tylenol, by Dioxin, by herpes, by AIDS, by a profusion of poisons which would come to dominate our group-fantasies. Then, like Frosch's patient, we would have a "psychotic insight" into where all this poison was coming from. We would become convinced that there was one central source of evil, and that a worldwide conspiracy was spreading the poison into "hot spots" around the globe which were dangerous to our body politic. Our delusion would then enter its final grandiose stage. We would believe it was our mission to save the world. We would instruct our leader to attack this dangerous poisoner in whatever guise he might appear, even in seemingly unthreatening places, to prevent the apocalypse which was about to overwhelm the world.

Beginning in the summer of 1982, America would sink more and more into overt paranoid group-fantasies. Led by a group of men who believed the biblical apocalypse was near, from Ronald Reagan, who believed America was under attack by "an evil force that would extinguish the light we've been tending for 6,000 years," to Caspar Weinberger, who believed that "the world is going to end as in the Book of Revelations...by an act of God...every day I think that time is running out,"[35] America foreign policy was becoming more and more divorced from reality. During 1982, the White House began playing "worldwide nuclear war games" for the first time since 1956, with

Apocalyptic fantasies began to proliferate.

Reagan, Weinberger, Bush and others directing nuclear exchange games while pretending they were flying safely above the holocaust.[36] It was after the first of these nuclear war games, during the summer of 1982, that Weinberger revealed new Pentagon plans "for fighting a long nuclear war"[37] which he said would be "far more survivable" than we had previously thought.

A year earlier, an army general had been fired for publicly saying that "the Soviets are on the move. They are going to strike."[38] But from the summer of 1982 on, Reagan and his aides all began openly making statements equally as paranoid, so that soon we all became so frightened that, as *The New Yorker* put it, "the first thing that people want to know when they turn on the news is...whether World War III has started."[39] Books on the coming apocalypse began selling in the millions,[40] and *Esquire* would soon report that "most Americans, says the Gallup poll, now think World War III may break out in the Eighties, that they themselves may not survive the attack, and that they would rather not think about the prospects."[41] As Senator David Pryor put it, "We are entering a period of sheer madness. It's time when the Unthinkable is becoming the Thinkable."[42]

What was "unthinkable" to a few, however, was not only thinkable but unconsciously *necessary* to most of America. War and even a nuclear holocaust provided places for us to dump our violent internal fantasies, and thus were *friends* of ours, poison containers into which our worst

Reagan said his best friend was an MX missile.

psychotic delusions could be dumped. As Reagan himself said, during a picture-taking session with his MX commission members, "Some of my best friends are MX missiles."[43] Without them we would feel overwhelmed by our internal anxieties, helpless to combat their terrifying content. Better to put our fantasies outside us, where, we hoped, they could be controlled in the deadly ritual of war.

Like the Aztecs, we would have to set up three sacrificial stages to provide for three group-fantasy levels:[44]

1. *Individual Sacrifice:* Individual men, women and children were regularly sacrificed by the Aztecs in cyclical rituals in order to feed the voracious gods and prevent the sun from becoming polluted. America decided to hold its individual sacrificial ritual in Lebanon, where unarmed Marines would be delegated as victims.

Since individual victims would not really cleanse us, only providing us with more evidence of further humiliation for our paranoid fantasies, we also would have to set up a second sacrificial stage.

2. *Mass Sacrifice:* In addition to individual sacrifices, the Aztecs would engage in sacred wars, including "Flower Wars" where their army fought tournaments amongst themselves solely to provide blood for the gods. America decided to hold its mass sacrificial wars in Central America and the Carribean, where we would send our youth into battle against "the international conspiracy."

Since enough victims to cleanse us still might not be produced by limited wars in Central America and the Caribbean, we would also have to ready a third sacrificial stage.

3. *Holocaust Sacrifice:* Despite all the victims provided by individual and mass sacrifices, the Aztec sun still built up so much pollution that every 52 years they had to go through a fantasied holocaust, an apocalyptic end of the world, which their New Fire Ceremony was supposed to act out. America decided to prepare Europe as the main stage for our holocaust sacrifice, should it be needed, in a group-fantasy that this would "clear up the bad blood" by destroying the source of the international conspiracy, and that America would be able to survive the nuclear war and enjoy the cleansed earth once again.

The sacrifice of individuals in Lebanon was relatively simple to set up. After a limited and well-defined mission in Beirut in August 1982 to supervise the withdrawal of PLO forces, the Marines were sent back into the warring city under pretexts so flimsy that the *New York Times* reported on them under such headlines as "Role Is Uncertain" and "Confusion Surrounds...Mission."[45] Just as in Teheran in early 1979, during the setting up of Carter's sacrificial stage, the security of the American embassy was kept insufficient as compared to other

The Marines were sent back into Beirut as sacrificial victims.

embassies, so, too, in Beirut the Marines were the only forces instructed to carry "unloaded weapons even during Condition One alerts, the highest state of alert."[46] Signs were posted outside their compound, in clear view of terrorist factions, saying "Unload weapons before entering compound,"[47] and American newspapers at the time printed the sacrificial invitation in bold headlines:

MARINES IN E. BEIRUT
Unloaded Guns Carried On Patrol

United States Marines carrying unloaded machine guns, rifles and pistols entered East Beirut for the first time yesterday...The marines in Lebanon do not carry loaded weapons...[48]

To further assure the sacrifice, 350 Marines were told to sleep together in a single building on top of an ammunition depot— rather than spread out as did other forces in the city— and were not allowed to build the usual "S-shaped" barricades which would slow down terrorist vehicles before reaching the building in which they slept.[49]

Setting up the mass sacrificial stage in Central America and the Caribbean would take much more planning if we were to avoid guilt over starting the war, guilt which was encoded in media language as "the Vietnam

War in Central America was sexually exciting (fire), but we had to avoid guilt over starting it (Vietnam syndrome.)

syndrome." Once we could accept the delusion that Central America and the Caribbean were not only part of the conspiracy *but were also capable of poisoning us,* we could "overcome the Vietnam syndrome" and have our mass sacrifice there.

Such a delusional conviction would not be easy to bring about. There was little new going on in Central America that had not been present in earlier years when we had paid no attention to the area and felt quite unthreatened by what was happening there. Reagan himself, when asked earlier, "Can you just envision any circumstances under which we would be sending U.S. combat troops to El Salvador?'' thought the idea so laughable that he answered, "Well, maybe if they dropped a bomb on the White House I might get mad." Central American countries were simply too small to take seriously by anyone who was sane on the issue.

In a series of articles, public speeches and radio broadcasts in the summer of 1982, psychohistorian Casper Schmidt predicted that America would be ready to go to war against Nicaragua by the end of 1983, basing his analysis on American group-fantasies contained in the media and public opinion polls.[50] American excitement during the invasion of the

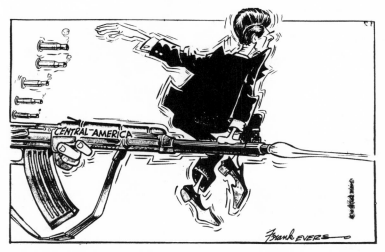

Reagan began to get excited about war in Central America.

Falklands, he argued, represented both a rehearsal and an authorization for future American invasion. The most likely area for the war would be Nicaragua and Honduras, where, he pointed out, cartoonists had already begun showing our intentions and military officers had already begun mapping out for Congress how such a plan could be accomplished. One army officer described in September 1982 to the House Committee on Foreign Affairs how "One possible scenario for the outbreak of a conflict between Nicaragua and Honduras" might be that "Sandinista troops or militia are in hot pursuit of a counter-revolutionary group that is escaping back into Honduras . . . they will likely confront a unit of the Honduran Regular Army. That confrontation would be an act of war...Such a war could easily spark off a regional conflagration involving all the nations of Central America, and perhaps the U.S."[51]

Nicaragua would be an ideal place to locate our paranoid fantasies. Since the purpose of the war would be to wipe out our own sexual vitality and our feelings about our on-going revolutionary changes in lifestyle, we would have to go to war against people very much like ourselves, people involved in their own revolutionary social experiments. Nicaragua was the Central American country most like America. It was a country which was, according to *The Boston Globe*, a "serious, popular, mostly well-intentioned and frequently competent national experiment not altogether unlike our own revolution."[52] Killing Nicaraguans would be like beating up Berkeley students, our own sons, so much like us. We could first identify with their revolutionary vitality and then wipe them out to kill these desires in ourselves. For Reagan personally, it would be like killing in himself the revolutionary seventeen-year-old "Dutch" Reagan who led the 1928 student rebellion which had successfully ousted the President of Eureka College.[53]

Militarily, we had to import enough violence into the area to produce turmoil in the fragile institutions of each country and to justify our group-fantasy that there was what the State Department called "a conspiratorial outside power" which was "destabilizing our hemisphere...from the Panama Canal to Mexico on our southern border," and which was about to threaten our borders.[54] To do this, we first moved to the Central American desks at the State Department seventeen out of eighteen of the most important people who had dealt with Vietnam during the Vietnam War.[55] We then began pouring military equipment into the hands of what even *Time* called "motley bands of rebels"[56] and death-squad leaders in several countries, counting on them to produce violence in the region. Like the violence-prone father who leaves loaded guns around the house and then feigns shock when his son uses them, we were not really surprised when much of the weaponry we sent to El Salvador ended up in rebel hands. Nor were we upset when the *contras* blew up civilian targets in Nicaragua—just as long as violence was created outside us, making the paranoid fantasies inside our heads feel more real. Marines pretended to invade an island which everyone knew was meant to be Grenada "to save American hostages," practicing on the island of Vieques near Puerto Rico in a naval exercise known as Ocean Venture 81. We had to be ready to attack "the international conspiracy" which had "the head of an octopus" in Moscow with "tentacles" in Cuba and the Caribbean and "tips of tentacles" in Central America. All these countries were in fact so small they posed no real threat to a country like America, whose power was literally millions of times greater than theirs. Invading them would be like the case of an abusive father who viciously beats up his four-year-old boy "because he said 'fuck you' to me."[57] Yet this type of psychotic thinking was precisely what was becoming an everyday occurrence beginning in 1982 for much of America. When *The Washington Post* headlined an article "New Dangers, Opportunities...Central America Seethes,"[58] the real meaning was "America Seethes with New Dangers and sees Opportunities to dump them into Central America."

For the first time since 1963, cartoonists began picturing Fidel Castro as being able to destroy the United States, this time through Central

Cuba was seen as possessing the power of destroying the United States through Central America.

America, and thousands of articles and books began appearing claiming that various groups in Central America and the Caribbean were part of a worldwide conspiracy that was intimately threatening us in various ways. The delusion would take time to spread, but eventually most Americans would believe it implicitly.

Like the Aztecs, America had been preparing its holocaust sacrificial ritual for several decades. By 1982, the main psychological condition for the holocaust had already been accomplished—a shared belief by most people in the central delusion that nuclear war was survivable. The scientific evidence against such a belief was overwhelming. Most scientists had agreed for some time that a nuclear exchange involving only a fraction of the 50,000 nuclear warheads that existed would kill hundreds of millions of human beings, and more recent studies have showed that the explosion of as few as 1,000 missiles would produce a radioactive "nuclear winter" that could easily end all photosynthesis and kill all human life on earth.[59] Therefore, *all* discussions and actions involving "nuclear options" and "limited nuclear exchanges" required psychotic thinking, under the delusion that those holding the discussion would survive. The fantasy is the same one which many individuals have when committing suicide, imagining how good they will feel watching their families come to their funerals. Fantasies of surviving one's own death and being "cleansed" by the experience—all "badness" being removed by death—are very common in suicidal individuals.[60]

Every aspect of current American nuclear strategy, every new warhead produced and deployed anywhere in the world, required the delusion that most Americans would "prevail in a limited nuclear exchange," as official Pentagon policy statements phrased it.[61] Reagan's 1983 Budget promised America could "successfully fight [a] nuclear war." Reagan himself, when asked if America could survive a nuclear war, replied that it could: "It would be a survival of some of your people and some of your facilities and you could start again."[62] So, too, public opinion polls showed that the majority of Americans shared the delusion that they would probably survive a limited nuclear war.[63]

Setting up the holocaust sacrifice would take longer to accomplish. Since it would involve too much guilt for either America or Russia to simply start a war out of the blue, war would have to be brought about by some other means. To date, conventional wars had been started by delegating the initial attack to a more impulse-prone group, so setting off the initial nuclear explosions would also have to be delegated to such a group. There were three main ways of accomplishing this delegation: (1) by allowing terrorists to get nuclear bombs, (2) by putting nuclear bombs in the hands of impulsive Third World countries and (3) by reducing the reaction time to a nuclear strike to just a few minutes, less time than a human needs to respond reliably, so that computers, pre-programmed to react "impulsively," could begin the holocaust.

Getting nuclear bombs into the hands of terrorists was the simplest task. Atomic bombs can be made from as little as four pounds of enriched plutonium. By proliferating unnecessary nuclear facilities and leaving them relatively unprotected, we have in the past three decades allowed tens of thousands of pounds of enriched uranium and plutonium to be stolen and unaccounted-for from American facilities alone.[64] There is also little question that terrorists are able to buy the technology needed to produce crude nuclear bombs from this material.

In addition, according to the most recent study on terrorist use of nuclear weapons, *The First Nuclear World War*,

> Stolen nuclear bombs, mostly artillery shells taken from European arsenals, are also available for a price...thirty-odd thousand U.S. nuclear bombs are stored in as many as two hundred domestic locations in forty states and several more in

Europe...security around U.S. nuclear weapons is apparently lax enough to warrant significant concern...In 1979 journalist Joseph Albright testified that by posing as a fencing contractor he was allowed into two Strategic Air Command bomb depots in late 1977. He came "within a stone's throw of four...nuclear weapons" while slowly riding in a jeep driven by a soldier (who had both hands on the wheel) armed only with a pistol. Albright noted that his briefcase was not searched before he toured the bomb storage areas, and he was allowed to keep it with him. He was later able to obtain by mail complete blueprints showing the depot's layout, a method of disabling the alarms, and the locations of two unguarded gates through the inner-most security fence.[65]

The "carelessness" required to "lose" tens of thousands of pounds of fissionable material and complete atomic warheads is exactly equivalent to the so-called "carelessness" of adults who habitually leave loaded guns or poisons near little children—that is to say, it is motivated, not accidental. It is not surprising, therefore, that there have already been at least 65 terrorist threats to use nuclear weapons in the U.S. alone.[66] How many of these involved real bombs remains a highly classified secret.

Making nuclear bombs available to Third World countries has required a much larger effort, involving shipment to these countries of enormnous amounts of nuclear facilities and material from which they can make nuclear warheads. In January of 1980, when asked about his coming policy on nuclear proliferation, Reagan had said: "I just don't think it is any of our business," and during his term he had reversed many of Carter's Nuclear Non-Proliferation Act policies, allowing, for instance, the shipment of U.S.-enriched spent fuel rods and the export of reprocessing technology, even to nations like Argentina, which has openly stated that it intends to make nuclear weapons.[67] Such stepped-up exportation of nuclear equipment, fuel and technology—much of it financed by multi-billion-dollar American contributions to the Export-Import Bank—guarantees that countries such as Argentina, Iraq, Iran, Libya, Taiwan and South Korea will soon join India, Israel, South Africa and Pakistan as nations with nuclear weapons. Once this is accomplished, local wars between Third World countries—wars which have been increasing in frequency in the past decade due to stepped-up arms shipments by the major powers—can produce the first nuclear explosion. This, in turn, under any one of dozens of scenerios, could escalate into the full holocaust.

Since each of America's thirty-one Poseidon submarines has enough warhead capacity to destroy all two hundred eighteen Soviet cities of one hundred thousands population, deterrence alone could be accomplished by having only a few submarines beneath the sea. Yet it would be wrong to conclude from this that all the remaining thousands of missiles, including the new MXs, cruise missiles and Pershing 2s, are aggressive

The world seemed dominated by the nuclear vulture.

America imagined Reagan as a vulture sitting on human bones.

weapons, motivated by macho display or redundant "overkill" purposes. In fact, their purpose is solely *suicidal*, not aggressive at all. The reaction time to Pershing 2 and cruise missiles is about six minutes. Bringing the reaction time down so low produces such a hair-trigger situation that, according to one member of the House defense task force, "most probably, the Russians will have to give a computer the authority to launch...whenever the computer thinks it perceives a United States launch."[69] In addition, putting the new missiles into Europe would encourage the Russians to put their SS20s and new cruise missiles even closer to Europe and the U.S., into Eastern Europe, into northern areas close to the U.S. and into submarines in the Atlantic. This, of course, would reduce *our* reaction time to a few minutes, making it likely that we, too, will give a computer the authority to trigger the holocaust. The day will soon come when both the Soviet Premier and the American President—and of course the heads of all European countries—will be only pretending to have control over the holocaust.

Setting the stage for the holocaust sacrifice by reducing reaction time to just a few mintues is often talked about as an "accidental" nuclear war. This is like calling the death of a little child "accidental" after the parent carefully places it on the edge of a cliff to play. In both cases the reduction of reaction time below that required to prevent disaster *is* the decision to produce the disaster. Thus, putting Pershing 2 and cruise missiles into Europe *is* the decision to begin the holocaust sacrifice. And since NATO military experts have recently said they can now easily stop a conventional Soviet attack on Europe without using nuclear weapons—as one NATO expert put it, "We have the technology to run circles around the Soviets"[70]—the placement of these new missiles is *nothing but* suicidal. Both the Americans who want the missiles there and the Europeans who agree to receive them are members of the older psychoclasses, sharing common anxieties about too much prosperity, personal freedom and sexuality in recent decades. Both are the same older psychoclasses who produced European wars every generation for centuries. Both imagine a holocaust will cleanse the world of evil forces, rather as World War II cleansed Europe for postwar renewal. And both share the delusion that they will survive the holocaust.

In order for Reagan's America to set the three sacrificial stages successfully, the most important condition would be to keep our real wishes from reaching consciousness, since it is only *unconscious* wishes which are compulsively acted out, beyond the reach of reality testing. Ronald Reagan—who, according to the polls, was turning out to be one of America's most effective fantasy leaders of the century—knew intuitively just how to bring about the sacrifices needed without making our real wishes conscious. We first would need a renewal of prosperity, producing new fears about too much poisonous pleasure building up. We would then need a formal announcement of who the enemy was, and some humiliating incidents and martyrs to prove how threatening the enemy was. Finally, we would need an authorization by the American people for the sacrificial war.

For Ronald Reagan, used to carrying out so many of his parents' unconscious desires, the grisly task which we would require of him in the months to come would be a labor of love.

7

THE POISON BUILDS UP

"There's a Virus in our Bloodstream"

By the fall of 1982, Reaganomics had completed its task of undoing the economic advances of recent years. Following the advice of the Chairman of the President's Council for Economic Advisers—"Don't stand there, undo something"— the dismantling of our Carter era prosperity had been fully accomplished and the sacrifice of the 150,000 victims of the recession was proceeding on schedule.[1]

Our ability to slow down the economy so thoroughly in less than two years was astonishing. One-third of America's productive capacity lay idle; over 12 million people (10.8 percent) were out of work, most with no unemployment benefits; real Gross National Product was dropping at a rate of 2 percent a year; over 2 million were homeless, many living in cars and tents along the road; over 40 million workers had lost their medical benefits; spending for child nutrition was cut by over $5 billion, pushing more than one in five children into poverty and raising infant death rates in areas worst affected by unemployment and federal cutbacks; government borrowing soared to $200 billion a year, a rate which would triple the national debt by the end of the decade; personal savings had dropped rather than increased as promised; businesses were failing at a far higher rate than in the 1930s; the foreign trade deficit was running over $4 billion a month; bank failures were triggering fears of a global collapse.[2] Reagan had done the job we had hired him to do. "What has been done so far, has been working very successfully," he told the country.[3] "The President seems . . . to be enjoying the job," said *Time*. " 'He is at peace with himself,' says White House Chief of Staff James Baker."[4]

The American people felt that their leader had done his job well. The majority of voters polled before the 1982 elections rated Reagan as "good" or "excellent" on the economy. Another poll found that he was "the favorite American of all time," just ahead of Abraham Lincoln. One reporter, interviewing unemployed workers as they went into the voting booths, was told: "Well, Reagan said it was going to be painful. It *is* painful, but the pain will do some good." Another put it even more positively. "This recession has been a cleansing thing," he said, with relief.[5] On "Nightline," reporter Ted Koppel, interviewing a clergyman on Christmas eve whose church had fed thousands of hungry families out of work, asked him whether the recession might not be "a good thing," since it had helped the faithful "rediscover their Christian goals."[6]

Johnny Carson captured the public's approval for Reaganomics best in his opening monologue:

> Carson: The Senate cut one million people off the food
>   stamp rolls yesterday.
> Audience: [Wild cheering, applause and laughter.]
> Carson: Let's hear it from the *truly mean* . . .

The response of professional economists to the total failure of Reagan's economic program to revitalize the country was two-fold. Most economists simply denied the reality and pronounced Reaganomics a success. As one put it: "After two years in power, President Reagan's Administration has made a miraculous improvement in the financial stability of the United States."[7] Those who could allow themselves to face the totality of the failure of Reagan's promise to produce "robust growth and a balanced budget" concluded that only Reagan had wanted Reaganomics. It was solely his fault, they said, because the entire country and all of Congress had been charmed by him against their will into approving the program. As the lead article on October 24, 1982 in *The New York Times Magazine* put it:

> Mr. Reagan's painless means to economic recovery has failed to deliver on its promise of simultaneous low inflation, robust growth and a balanced budget.
>
> How could the nation have gone from hope to gloom in less than two years? . . . How could Mr. Reagan's economic plan have been enacted in the first place? . . . Mr. Reagan's closest friend on Capitol Hill, [Senator] Laxalt, [said], "If there had been a secret ballot in the Senate last year, there wouldn't have been more than 12 votes for the tax cut."

The Senator's astonishing statement passed without comment at the Cabinet Room, [yet] his words are worth pondering. Given all the misgivings about the program, how could it have happened?

Recently, in dozens of interviews with The New York Times, central figures in the Administration and Congress have explored that question . . . running through all the comments of those interviewed was the image of a charming, insistent President—politically skilled, ideologically stubborn, a man who defied the odds and bent the public and the Government to his will.[8]

This, too, was why we had hired Ronald Reagan—to take all the guilt upon himself for the blood of the sacrificial victims. He alone had "bent us to his will."

Reagan played his part well. Having alone caused the economic disaster, he alone could now save us from it. Since the tax cuts and the strangulation of the money supply had created the recession, a tax increase and a sudden expansion of the money supply could save us at the brink of total collapse. Both of these miracles were easily accomplished. "The truth is," Reagan said, "we've . . . accomplished a minor miracle. We've pulled America back from the brink of disaster."

Reagan saved us from the brink of disaster.

Reagan was hailed as our savior, and within a few months the economy began to respond, as it had done so many times before, with signs of recovery. The Federal Reserve Bank, which until that time had been pulling money out of circulation, now let the money supply grow at an annual rate of 15 percent, allowing its discount rate for bank borrowing to drop to 8.5 percent by year's end, the lowest rate since 1978. We had decided America was not to have a Great Depression after all.

Reagan's decision to end the recession had an immediate effect on the stock market and on the mood of the nation. Cartoons in the fall of 1982 showed people floating in the air, as joyous as were the Aztecs who saw the new bonfires, indicating that the old polluted heart had been ripped out of the

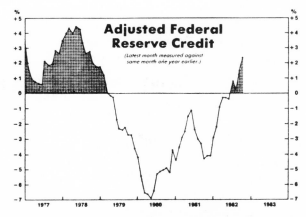

The economic sun rose above the horizon.

sacrificial victim and a new heart had been put in its place. In fact, the group-fantasy that we had been given a new heart was so strong that

People floated in the air on hearing of the end of the internal sacrifice.

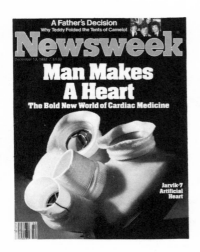

Like the Aztecs, we made a new heart.

when surgeons put an artificial heart into Barney Clark, we followed his "recovery" in front-page headlines and special TV programs—imagining, like the Aztecs, that every beat of his artificial heart would pump new, unpolluted blood into our body politic.[9] It did not matter that economic reality lagged far behind our fantasy of instant recovery. The media soon stopped reporting stories on the hungry and homeless—one reporter wondered why "the 'new poor' and homeless discovered by the press a few months ago seem to have vanished"[10]—and concentrated instead on Barney Clark's miraculous new heart. Perhaps the world could be renewed, perhaps our polluted national bloodstream could be cleansed through the internal sacrifice alone. Perhaps we would not need a war to feel reborn.

We soon realized it was not to be so simple. Even the Great Depression of the Thirties couldn't drain off all our poisonous feelings and required the blood sacrifice of the Second World War to really cleanse us.[11] Like Frosch's paranoid patient, once we began to slide into the psychotic process, our punitive superego more and more took control of our fantasy life, and every pleasure in life began to be seen as "poisonous." Our national superego—which a year earlier we had pictured as a disapproving "laser eye" Supreme Judge watching us—now declared that our newly reviving economic life was "poisonous" to our body politic. Poison group-fantasies proliferated in the media. *The New York Times* reported that "many Americans keep saying, it's a poison in the body politic,"[12] *The New York Post* imagined there was "poison oozing from the White House,"[13] and Reagan announced that "This Administration hereby declares an all-out war on [those] who are poisoning our young people."[14]

The poisoning group-fantasy was often projected into the Soviets, as when they were accused of poisoning Asians with "yellow rain" chemical toxins, which scientists had

We imagined poison "yellow rain" in the air around us.

long ago shown to have been only bee excrement.[15] More often, however, it was our own economy which was used to convey our poisoning fantasies, either directly—as when Reagan likened the economy to "a poisonous gas" or as when Martin Feldstein was said to believe that a jobs program for the unemployed would "poison the economy"[16]—or in images of sickness, as when Reagan announced to the nation on October 13th that the economy was suffering from an "out-of-control disease" which he said was like "a virus in our bloodstream."

Of course, Reagan had for decades used poison and disease imagery in his description of our national condition, from his fears that welfare was a "spreading cancer" to his notion that *trees* had caused "92 percent of the air pollution in this country,"[17] confusing nitrous oxide and oxides of nitrogen in his mind in order to convey his basic conviction that there were poisons surrounding him which he couldn't do anything about, since they came from his own projections. That Reagan was preoccupied with disease was even recognized by his film directors, who usually cast him as ill, giving him pneumonia in *Knute Rockne*, epilepsy in *Night Unto Night*, anthrax in *Stallion Road*, amputated legs in *King's Row* and alcoholism in *Dark Victory* and other films. Because of his phobias, he was closely identified with body illness. As his film biographer notes, "his best and most memorable performances were when he was ill."[18]

Whenever nations have gone a long time since their last sacrificial cleansing, they choose a leader who easily entertains paranoid poison fantasies. The basic group-fantasy of every nation is that its leader functions as a literal "poison container" for its emotions. When he is seen as strong, early in his term, the nation feels safe, but when he is felt to be weak, during his "collapse" phase, the nation itself feels in danger of becoming poisoned, because he can no longer contain all the poisons being dumped into him. When nations have not had a sacrifice for some time, they imagine themselves to be particularly full of poison, especially when they are coming out of an economic slump and the renewed national vitality threatens to produce dangerous new pleasures. Such was the fantasy, for instance, just before the Second World War, when President Roosevelt told America in a speech that we couldn't let Jews or other European

Reagan was seen as a poison container into which we dumped our emotions.

We put so much poison into Reagan that we imagined he smelled bad.

refugees into our country because Europe was full of "fifth columnists and saboteurs which were undiluted poison that must not be allowed to spread in the New World."[19] So, too, the economic expansion just before Vietnam produced a "Pollution Alert" scare at the end of 1963, when the head of the U.S. Public Health Service imagined that "pollution was growing considerably from the threat of epidemic disease being imported into the U.S. from abroad."[20] The renewed vitality of the American economy at the end of 1982 produced The Great Reagan Poison Alert, when for six months the media was dominated by fears of disease and poisons of all sorts, real and imaginery, usually connected with fantasies of punishment for sexuality.

The opening gun of the Poison Alert was a sensationalized *Time* cover story on the herpes virus, featuring a blood-red "Herpes" on the

Herpes was seen as our punishment for sex.

cover and containing the most horrifying stories that could be found on the "incurable" effects of herpes, concluding that "perhaps not so unhappily, it may be a prime mover to bring to a close an era of mindless promiscuity."[21] For the next two months, the entire press and TV corps seemed to have become addicted to herpes scare stories, usually ending in a tone of "it serves us right" for having too much sexual freedom. "Will Herpes Bring Back Morality To America?" asked a *Reader's Digest* cover.[22] "Is Disease Shaping a New Sexual Ethic?" asked *Mother Jones*.[23] America was portrayed as hopelessly lustful, and herpes was thought to be the modern plague sent by God to punish us for our sexual excesses. No mention was made of the fact that herpes had been around since Roman times, or that the current version had been widespread for several years without attracting media attention, or that new antiviral medications promised control of the disease. As our economy revived—and as we reduced our sacrificial offerings (the unemployed) which had drained us of our sins so far—we needed a place to put our fantasies that dangerous poisons were building up inside us, and herpes provided a perfect container for these fantasies.

The same explanation holds for the spate of articles that fall claiming that America was militarily weaker than the Soviet Union. The connection between fears of bodily disease and fears of American weakness and communist strength have been common knowledge ever since Col. Jack D. Ripper launched the holocaust in the movie *Dr. Strangelove* because "the commies were poisoning our precious bodily fluids." Col. Ripper discovered the communist poisoning plot which had so weakened America "during the act of physical love." When Reagan gave address after address to the American people armed with charts which were distorted to show that Russia had more and bigger missiles than we did, he was voicing the same paranoid fears of impotence as Col. Ripper's.

Most Americans agreed with Reagan's claims that our national phallus had been shrinking lately, despite all evidence to the contrary. During Reagan's "collapse" phase, we were seized by a hysterical epidemic similar to the one Asians call "koro," where the men in large areas of the country suddenly believe that their penises are shrinking and come running into hospitals holding on to their penises with a string, lest they disappear into their abdomens.[25] Like Col. Ripper, and like Frosch's paranoid patient, we felt we were being weakened by *something*, and felt that this something (really our own sexuality, our own desires for pleasure, our own revived hopefulness) was becoming more and more poisonous to us each day.

The way large groups usually objectify these vague poisoning fears is to delegate to individuals the task of acting out what is feared, so it can be seen to exist "out there" in what can be called "reality," rather than remain only inside. During Carter's "collapse" phase, we delegated Rev. Jim Jones to act out our poisoning fantasies for us in Jonestown.[26] Four years later, in September of 1982, during Reagan's "collapse" phase,

Jonestown acted out our poison fantasies during the Carter "collapse" phase.

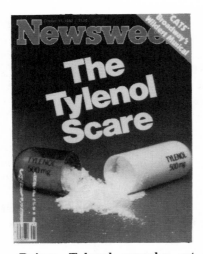

Poison Tylenol capsules set off The Great Reagan Poison Alert.

several local poisoning incidents began breaking out in the Middle West—the largest being a milk poisoning scheme in Cedar Rapids, Iowa[27]—but these were not reported nationally because no one died from them. On September 30th, one finally succeeded, in Chicago, killing seven people with poison which was put into Tylenol capsules. The Great Reagan Poison Alert was on in earnest.

Each element of the Tylenol poisonings could be traced to earlier elements in our national group-fantasy. The poison used was cyanide, the same as had been used in poisoning the purple Koolade drink in Jonestown. The Tylenol bottle was the same as the popular "Reaganol" bottles sold in stores across the country containing jellybeans marked "Temporary relief from inflationary anxiety . . . package not child-resistant." Even the jellybeans might have been linked in the poisoner's mind to the story in *Time* citing Reagan as saying, as he swallowed a purple jellybean, "they tell me the purple ones are poison."[28]

The "Death Pill" was often shown next to Reagan's picture.

In any case, the press underlined the link between Reagan and the Tylenol poisoning wherever it could. The press vividly depicted a "Tylenol Scare in the White House" as "grim-faced secret service agents fanned out through the White House removing bottles of Extra-Strength Tylenol soon after seven people died" and by running headlines on the "Death Pill Peril" next to Reagan's picture.[30] When the main suspect for the Tylenol poisonings, James Lewis, later was discovered to have sent a death threat to Reagan,[31] somehow it seemed appropriate to our group-fantasy that Reagan—and America—was being poisoned.

By the end of 1982, there were so many poison alerts that it seemed as though America had become a giant Jonestown. More poison Tylenol was discovered in Illinois; cyanide was found in Anacin tablets in California; in Colorado, someone put mercuric chloride into Excedrin tablets and rat poison into Anacin capsules; in Wyoming, hydrochloric acid was found in Visene eye drops; in Minneapolis, sodium hydroxide was put into chocolate milk; in Louisiana, one town found cyanide in its water supply; in Florida, someone put insecticide into an orange juice container.[32]

By Halloween, literally hundreds of people were swept up into acting out the group-fantasy, this time on children begging for candy in "trick or treat" visits. Stimulated by newspaper headlines such as "TRICK OR TERROR—Nationwide Poison Candy Alert: Keep Kids At Home,"[33] impulse-ridden individuals put hundreds of different poisons into candy, Demerol into cookies, pins into apples and razor blades into frankfurters in order to make our internal fears concrete. Russell Baker captured the feeling of The Great Reagan Poison Alert in his *New York Times* column:

> For five weeks I travelled across beautiful autumnal America. It was like a booby hatch of the criminally insane.
>
> In Detroit they were finding razor blades in hot dogs sold at the grocery. In California somebody had laced eyewash with corrosive chemicals. In Chicago, capsules sold as headache remedies came packed with cyanide. In New York and its suburbs, not to be outdone, people spent the weekend inserting needles and pins into candy they planned to give children on Halloween . . .
>
> I was struck by the sense of encroaching madness . . .[35]

Like Frosch's paranoid patient, descending into the depths of his psychosis, Reagan's America felt surrounded by poisoners—only in our group-fantasy we delegated concrete poisoning episodes to impulsive individuals within the nation to make our feelings seem more "real."

For the next three months, the news media were dominated by poison alert stories. As the poison pill and food stories subsided, they were replaced by headlines and cartoons of environmental poisoning. As one cartoonist saw it, we felt as if we were in Noah's ark. The flood was subsiding (the recession was ending) and we wanted to step out on dry, safe

We felt our world was full of poison.

land . . . but found that instead of the flood having cleansed the world, it had left it full of poison!

In actuality, America was much *less* polluted in the 1980s than in the 1960s and early 1970s, due to the dramatic effects of hundreds of recent environmental programs. Yet the press now suddenly discovered that our environment was being polluted beyond anything we had yet experienced, and a full media blitz, complete with scare headlines and TV specials, focused on the remaining problem areas. All of America seemed like a "HOUSE THAT DIED OF POISON," as the *Daily News* phrased it, as hundreds of reporters were sent out to find any "poison" story which might allow them to reflect our internal emotions.

In only one sense did these stories have some relation to reality. It was

"The House That Died of Poison"

true that the Reagan administration—hoping to make the environment match their own feelings of sinful pollution—had attempted to reverse many of the government's recent environmental programs. As Ralph Nader put it, "They want to kill everything off. They want to destroy the OSHA [Occupational Safety and Health Administration], auto safety, environmental health . . . within two years, they'll be known as the Cancer Party."[36] Even so, most of Reagan's "deregulation" efforts were only partly effective, the environment as a whole remained far less polluted than before, and such continuing problems as dioxin, nuclear waste and acid rain were all that remained to convey our paranoid feelings of being poisoned from within. Headlines reading "THE ENEMY BELOW"[37] and "NEW

DIOXIN 'HOT SPOT' IS DISCOVERED''[38] were merged in our minds with others showing global maps of "THE WORLD'S HOT SPOTS" (places of armed conflict), until we hardly knew from one page.to the next if the dangerous "hot spots" (sexuality) were inside us (THE ENEMY BELOW), around us (DIOXIN HOT SPOT) or overseas (WORLD'S HOT SPOTS). The American Medical Association, reacting to such scare headlines as "TOXIC CHEMICAL ALL AROUND US, SCIENTISTS SAY," finally issued a statement saying that "experts have yet to document a single death" from dioxin, pointing out that "the news media has made dioxin the focus of a witch hunt by disseminating rumors, hearsay and unconfirmed, unscientific reports" which generated "unjustified public fright and hysteria."[41]

James Watt was felt to be poisoning us.

"Hysteria" it indeed was. But mere scientific statements could not change our deepest feelings. We needed something to dramatize our conviction that we were being poisoned by too much pleasure. Something like herpes, but far more deadly.

The government was seen awash in poison.

For a time, we played with the hope that we could objectify these feelings by running stories of the "chemical castration" of rapists, where judges for the first time tried giving rapists the choice between long jail terms and injections of Depo-Provera, which supposedly lowered their sexual desires.[42] Yet even though this news story linked the "poisonous" injections to punishment for sex, it was too limited in scope to make a really powerful group-fantasy. What we needed was something felt to be all around us, something we all could get, something that could be directly seen as a punishment for sexual excess. What we needed was an antisexual epidemic.

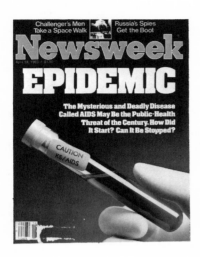

We felt we had a poison blood epidemic.

The epidemic we found was AIDS, the usually fatal Acquired Immune Deficiency Syndrome. Not only was AIDS mysterious, without a known cause, but it mainly affected "promiscuous homosexuals," which the New Right had been warning since Reagan's election would be the cause of terrible disasters for America. The problem was, explained the *National Review*, that homosexuals had recently broken their pact with all of us to stay out of sight and not stir up our homosexual feelings. "Homosexuals committed to fighting openly for their civil liberties are asking for it," they said.[43] Homosexuals who dared to demonstrate for more help for AIDS victims soon found themselves faced with anti-homosexual counter-demonstrations, with frightened, angry people carrying signs saying "DON'T DESTROY AMERICA WITH YOUR LUST." Soon the fantasy that AIDS was contracted from "contaminated blood" spread around the country,[44] reaching the deepest fear anyone can have, a fear which goes all the way back to the time in the womb when each of us was actually poisoned from time to time by the inability of our own placenta to cleanse the waste in our bloodstream.[45] The "poison blood" group-fantasy was so frightening that hospital workers refused to touch the "poisonous" blood of AIDS victims, medical technicians began using gloves when touching anyone who was bleeding, equipment touched by homosexuals was thrown away, morticians refused to bury AIDS victims, and blood donations dropped off dangerously due to fears of "infected needles."[46] In local meetings all across the country, homosexuals were denounced publicly as "rapists . . . sinners and liars," people who held orgies in "sex clubs," people who "because of AIDS" endangered everyone in the community.[47] "A lot of people feel that gays have gotten what they deserve," one worker told a *New York Times* reporter. "On a bulletin board next to him was a cartoon of a middle-aged woman airing her view on AIDS: 'Good Christian people have nothing to fear as long as we stay a million miles away from the slimy creatures who may have it.' "[49]

In fact, what "a lot of people" *really* felt was that gays had gotten what *we* deserved: an anti-sexual epidemic, a plague sent by God to punish us all for such things as the sexually explicit cable TV programs watched in millions of American homes.[49] "AIDS may mean the party is over,'' mused *Newsweek*, expressing our feelings by citing an anonymous homosexual as saying, ''Maybe we *are* wrong—maybe this is a punishment.''[50]

By February 1983, the Great Reagan Poison Alert reached its climax. Carter's ''collapse'' phase had peaked during the summer of 1979, with images of disintegration, strangulation and death. Reagan's ''collapse''

Reagan's ''collapse'' phase was dominated by images of disintegration and death.

phase peaked six months earlier in his term, with images of disintegration, disease and poisoned blood. Carter had responded to our distress by arranging for hostages to be taken in Teheran, giving us an external ''enemy'' to blame for our malaise. Reagan, however, seemed to be dragging his feet. When would he find us an enemy? We couldn't take all those free-floating poisoning fears indefinitely without having *someone* to blame them on.

The first to call Reagan to account on his broken promise to find us an enemy was the Right. William Safire, in a column headed ''REAGAN'S WHITE FLAG,'' told his *New York Times* readers that the President had surrendered his principles, ''had admitted failure and abandoned 'ideology.' ''[51] *The Times* itself echoed Safire and editorialized that ''The stench of failure hangs over Ronald Reagan's White House.''[52] Some columnists tried to reassure their readers that ''Reagan is not another Carter. He is tough. He is a leader.''[53] Yet polls showed Reagan's popularity had dropped to 10 points lower than even Carter's at midterm, lower than any president in American history at this point. John Lofton, in *The Washington Times*, felt Reagan was so impotent that he was not a man at all, but a dreaded *woman*, a ''political 'Tootsie' . . . wearing clothes quite frankly . . . I was unaware

Reagan was taunted with being a woman for not giving us an enemy to fight.

were in his wardrobe . . . he is now decked out . . . in a big floppy hat, a skirt, high heels, wearing bright red lipstick and carrying a purse."[54] It was time to show Reagan that the American people were more belligerent than he was.

Public opinion pollsters had earlier interviewed people on how willing they were to go to war. Under headlines such as "AMERICANS WILLING TO FIGHT, PROUD OF U.S.," they reported: "In case of war, 71 percent of the Americans said they would fight for their country," apparently regardless of where the war was fought, since that was not part of the question.[55] The message to Reagan was obvious. Even women reporters told Reagan they were more ready to go to war than he was. In Reagan's January 5th press conference, one woman reporter stood up and asked him a question about whether women might "go to war with the troops." Reagan was taken aback, and, confused, replied, "Sarah, I have to say that there's only one criteria, and that is if we're going to ask an American young man or woman—but I don't think we'll put the young women in those combat front ranks." Sarah shouted back at him: "WE'RE READY!" The whole press room roared with relief as she voiced our national plea.

By February, with Reagan still negligent in designating an enemy for us, the American press produced the greatest outpouring of "go to war" imagery that had been seen since just before Vietnam. Since most of the world was at peace, the words "DECLARE WAR" had to be hidden in whatever guise was at hand, producing such headlines as these:

A DECLARATION OF WAR (Common Cause ad)
REAGAN SHOULD COME OUT SHOOTING (Patrick
                                        Buchanan column)
IT'S WAR! ARMY VS. ROACH (*Daily News*)
FARMERS **DECLARE WAR** (*New York Post*)
RON TO CHURCH: **DECLARE WAR** ON NUKE FOES (*New
                                        York Post*)
DISTRICT **DECLARES WAR** ON RABIES (*Washington Post*)
IS WORLD **ON BRINK OF** TRADE **WAR**? (*U.S. News*)
THE **WAR** FOR CHINATOWN (*New York*)
IT LOOKS LIKE WAR AT THE PEACE CORPS (Jack Ander-
                                        son column)
THE **WAR** OF WORDS ON EUROMISSILES (*Daily News*)
PREZ GOES TO WAR FOR DEFENSE BUDGET (*New York
                                        Post*)
ARMY **BEEFS UP WAR** ON FATTIES (*New York Post*)
THE **WAR** ON KIDNEY STONES (*Daily News*)
OIL PRICE **WAR** (*Daily News*)
THE **COMING** TAX **WAR** (Joseph Kraft column)

A DECLARATION OF WAR

Reagan should come out shooting

IT'S WAR! Army vs. roach

Farmers declare war

RON TO CHURCH: DECLARE WAR ON NUKE FOES

District Declares War on Rabies

Is World on Brink Of Trade War?

THE WAR FOR CHINATOWN
By Michael Daly

It looks like war

The war of words

PREZ GOES TO WAR FOR DEFENSE BUDGET

ARMY BEEFS UP WAR ON FATTIES

THE WAR ON KIDNEY STONES

OIL PRICE WAR

The Coming Tax War

Strap on the guns, Dutch!

BANK WAR

Tuning in on 'The Winds of War'

Gays At War

GAYS **AT WAR** (*Mother Jones*)

STRAP ON THE GUNS, DUTCH! (Patrick Buchanan column)
BANK **WAR** ON INTEREST WITHHOLDING (Maxwell
Newton column)
TUNING IN ON 'THE WINDS OF **WAR**' (*New York Post*)
WAR INSIDE CITY COUNCIL (*Atlantic City*)
REAGAN DECLARES WAR ON THE MOB (*New York Post*)
THE WINDS OF **WAR** (*People*)
PREZ PLANS TV BLITZ IN FEDERAL **WAGE WAR** (*New
York Post*)
DRUNK-DRIVER **WAR SHIFTING INTO HIGH** (*Daily
News*)
WAR OF SECRETS (William Safire column)
YES, **UNCLE SAM MUST LEAD THE WAR** ON DRUGS
(Letter to the Editor)
BLOODLESS BUT BITTER **NEW WAR** BETWEEN THE
STATES (*Des Moines Sunday Register*)
POLS **GO TO WAR** IN SCHOOL BOARD ELECTIONS (*New
York Post*)
PREVENTION **BATTLE CRY OF** MDs IN **WAR** AGAINST
ALCOHOLISM (*Clinical Psychiatry News*)
MUGGERS **DECLARE WAR** ON ANGELS (*New York Post*)
THE RISING TIDES OF WAR (*Time*)
ALL-OUT **WAR DECLARED** ON MIDTOWN PARKERS
(*New York Post*)

Reagan could no longer mistake the urgency of our demand. He would
have to find us an enemy and prepare for war so we could shift the
poison abroad.

Not that he liked being pushed into it. At his February 16th press conference, one of the reporters asked him what his reaction was to the recent rumor that "his aides" were pushing him into decisions lately.
"Well, I'll tell you," he replied, angrily, "I read those things, too, and I
get pretty frustrated, because—maybe I'm going to have to have an exhibition up here in which we get some of those unnamed aides up and see
if they can push me off the platform! I'm not being pushed around . . .
there's no one pushing me . . ."

Our pushing, nevertheless, worked. Reagan gave three dramatic
speeches in March to announce (1) why we had to go to war (the March
8th "Evil Empire" speech), (2) whom we would have to invade (the
March 11th "Central America" speech) and (3) how we would handle
the guilt for our invasion (the March 23rd "Star Wars" speech.)

The "Evil Empire" speech was purely religious, labeled "Reagan in the Pulpit" by *The New York Times*.[56] In it, he told us that "there is sin and evil in the world, and we are enjoined by Scripture and our Lord Jesus to oppose it with all our might." After confusing the voice of the press with the voice of Jesus Christ, he then went on to confuse himself with the enemy. He cited C. S. Lewis:

> It was C. S. Lewis who, in his unforgettable *Screwtape Letters* wrote:
>
> "The greatest evil is not now done in those sordid 'dens of crime' that Dickens loved to paint . . . it is conceived and ordered (moved, seconded, carried, and minuted) in clear, carpeted, warmed, and well-lighted offices by quiet men with white collars and cut fingernails and smooth-shaven cheeks who do not need to raise their voice."
>
> Because these "quiet men" do not "raise their voices," because they sometimes speak in soothing tones of brotherhood and peace, [we are tempted to] ignore the facts of history and the aggressive impulses of an evil empire . . .

What Reagan was here describing was what he felt *himself*, sitting in his own "carpeted, warmed and well-lighted office," with his "white collar and cut fingernails," having to announce "without raising his voice" that we had to go to war—or, as he put it, had to "oppose evil with all our might." He had known all during his life-long crusade that this terrible moment must come. Though the world seemed quiet, it was all deception. It was time to act out "the struggle between right and wrong, good and evil," he said. It was time to fight the Evil Empire.

Reagan's second speech, on Central America, began by describing how the Soviets were now using Grenada, Cuba and Nicaragua as bases. This was the cause of the trouble in Central America and the Caribbean, he said, and now we were forced to step in and stop their growing threat. Having set up the immediacy of the danger, he then announced to the American people that we would eventually have to send combat troops to the area . . . announced it, that is, in the time-honored code Presidents use in announcing such things to the American people:

> Are we going to send American soldiers into combat? The answer is a flat no . . . Are we going to Americanize the war with a lot of U.S. combat advisors? Again the answer is no.

The effect was the same as when Lyndon Johnson stood before us and repeated over and over again that "no American combat troops would be sent to Vietnam." We knew the real meaning of the message, as clearly as the child knows what's really going on when daddy brings his pistol up from the basement, loads it and tells him he is *not* going to use it to shoot mommy. Shortly later, when asked about sending American troops, Reagan would change the "flat no" to "the President should never say never." Nevertheless, even then, on March 11th, we knew what he meant.

The March 23rd "Star Wars" speech was Reagan's masterpiece. It would be cited by the media hundreds of times in the coming months as the turning point in his foreign policy. The speech had two aims. It had to show that the Evil Empire was very close and was growing more dangerous by the minute, and it had to make us feel that if we got into war once again we would be safe from nuclear retribution.

The speech opened with Reagan's dramatic announcement that "I have reached a decision . . . a very important decision . . . to make America strong again . . ." While we had been neglecting our military, he explained, the Soviets had been producing twice as many combat aircraft, three times as many attack submarines, five times as many tanks, fourteen times as many artillery, and so on. Where had the Soviets put all these dangerous new weapons? Reagan brought out a series of giant, indistinct photographs. Look, the poisonous weapons were *right there* . . . he pointed to the photos . . . "in Western Cuba, we see this military airfield" . . . another photo showed "Soviet military hardware that has made its way to Central America" . . . a third showed "on the small island of Grenada . . . an airfield with a 10,000-foot runway. Grenada doesn't even have an air force. Who is it intended for?"

Reagan paused dramatically. It seemed obvious that the airport was dangerous to us. Overlooked for the moment was the fact that, according to *Aviation Weekly* and the British firm which designed it, it was only good for tourist planes, lacking the "facilities that would be needed for it to operate as a military base including such military requisites as underground fuel facilities, navigational and surveillance radar, underground weapons storage, parallel taxiways or dispersal sites and workshop and storage facilities for anything other than light twin-engine aircraft."[57] It *must be* dangerous, we felt, as we squinted at the dark photo flickering on our TV screen, like an inkblot into which we could project our fears. The poison seemed very close to us (even though Grenada was 1,500 miles from the tip of Florida.) Some of us had even vacationed at one of those "pleasure islands" in the Caribbean. We would have to keep a careful eye on Grenada. Small as it was, it was one of the "hot spots"—rather like dioxin, seemingly innocent, but working silently to poison us.

The second purpose of the "Star Wars" speech—promising an impregnable defense against a nuclear holocaust—appears at first glance to have little connection with Grenada and Central America, since these areas did not have nuclear weapons even if we should invade them. Yet, in the unconscious, Reagan's "Star Wars" fantasy of a screen around the U.S. which could stop all missiles made sense to us. We were, after all, planning to kill our persecutors. Like a paranoid individual who decides to attack his persecutors, we needed a fantasy that would protect us from retribution. Paranoid individuals sometimes hallucinate a "magic bubble" or a "plastic shield" which they think able to surround them, protecting them from their imagined enemies.

Reagan announced a Star Wars plan for fighting the enemy.

Reagan promised us that "we could intercept and destroy strategic ballistic missiles before they reach our own soil [and] give us the means of rendering these nuclear weapons impotent and obsolete." Imagine, being able to render the Soviets *impotent*. "Isn't it worth every investment," he asked excitedly. "We know it is!"

The "Star Wars" defense bubble idea, with its lasers and space stations and millisecond response time, had been kicking around the Pentagon for years without finding a backer. Carter's space weapons chief, Col. Robert M. Bowman, called it "the ultimate military lunacy, easily overwhelmed and vulnerable," which would give the nuclear holocaust "a hair-trigger of milliseconds."[58] Although Reagan said in his speech that his "very big decision" had been made "after careful consultation with my advisors, including the Joint Chiefs of staff," his own military hated the plan, and leaked a story the next day to *The Washington Post* which reported that the idea was Reagan's alone, and that he had "personally overruled objections from top Pentagon officials when he announced [it.]"[59] Yet in the end it was the emotional function of the defense shield that mattered, not the scientific facts. We were feeling so crazy by then we *had* to have an invulnerable shield. Let the scientists call it "insane," which they did.[60] Let experts say, like MIT's George Rathjens, that "the president—I hate to say this—on this issue is out of touch with reality."[61] Let people point out it would be destabilizing to the extreme, and that before long "the earth itself will have been turned into a gigantic orbiting bomb."[62] By now, most Americans were as out of touch with reality as Reagan. We *needed* this "space bubble" fantasy if we were to go to war. Reagan had, after all, made his "very big decision" to announce the "space shield" plan at the same moment he made his decision to oppose the Evil Empire. Both the defensive and the aggressive fantasies were inexorably linked together.

The emotional effects of these three speeches were electric. Reagan's sagging polls soared. He proudly proclaimed two days later that "a dark cloud had been lifted" from America.[63] The Great Reagan Poison Alert ended. Any further poison episodes—such as the 10 people killed by the sedative Zomax, which was made by the same firm as Tylenol—were now relegated to the back pages of newspapers.[64] Cartoonists stopped portraying the government as a poisoner. The "poison in our bloodstream" had all been dumped into Central America. Whereas in February, magazines showed a poisonous serpent in the womb of the

In February, the poisonous serpent was beneath us, but in March, after Reagan's speech, it was shown in Central America.

earth, beneath our cities, in March they showed the same poisonous serpents in Central America. Reagan had finally given us our enemy.

Soon the State Department began referring to the Nicaragua desk as the "Get Nicaragua Desk." A major new group-fantasy began to be elaborated that "a brown horde" of Latins were about to flood into the U.S. Reagan called it "a tidal wave of refugees," a fantasy identical to that of Roosevelt when he feared the "undiluted poison" which might pour into America from European refugees.[65] The images of poison in Central America took varied forms. Nicaragua was called "the tip of the tentacles of the poisonous Soviet octopus" or "a poison spider crawling up our leg," and Central America was seen to be "hemorrhaging people into the United States,"[66] even though refugee immigration was only one-third what it had been before Reagan was president. The "poison in our bloodstream'' wasn't coming from homosexuals after all, but from countries *below us*.

For a while, we actually felt much better for having dumped the poison abroad. We were like Frosch's patient, who felt better for a while after his "discovery" that his vague internal poisoning fears were due to a worldwide poisoning conspiracy. Our paranoid fears, however, would soon return. Delusional solutions usually

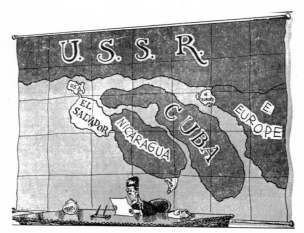

We felt we had dumped our poison into Nicaragua, Cuba and the USSR, making them bloated and threatening.

break down when supposed "enemies" become so threatening in our imagination that they have to be annihilated. It would not be long before we would have to take action against the Evil Empire of our waking dreams.

8

THE POISON IS DUMPED ABROAD

"There's a Fire in our Front Yard"

Once the enemy had been designated, Reagan's America lurched into its "upheaval" phase. The more Reagan prepared for war, the higher his polls climbed.[1] "He has Washington spooked," reported *Time*. "There has been nothing quite like this since Franklin Roosevelt." Visitors to America, they said, "would have thought Reagan was kind of a laid back god" from the support given his new get-tough policies.[2]

The media fueled the rising war hysteria with bellicose headlines. "REAGAN SOUNDS THE ALARM."[3] "HARDENING THE LINE."[4] "REAGAN HANGS TOUGH."[5] "NO MORE MR. NICE GUY."[6] "THE WRATH OF RON."[7] "A PLAN TO WIN IN EL SALVADOR."[8] Each headline was as much an incitement of Reagan as

We looked forward to "The Wrath of Ron."

it was a description of his actions. After the poison had built up inside us for so long, it felt terrific to have a place to dump it abroad. "We now have a program that has . . . unanimous support," Reagan told us, "support by the Congress and the American people. For this consensus will unite us . . . We can no longer afford to delay. The time to act is now."[9]

The call to "act now" felt extraordinarily liberating. Although little was happening in Central America that was new, Reagan now declared it was "a spiritual crisis" for the West. *The New Republic* reported Reagan as saying in one of his speeches, "The enemy without is Communism . . . which the President described as 'the focus of evil in the modern world;' the speech left friends and foes around the world with the impression that the President of the United States was contemplating holy war."[10]

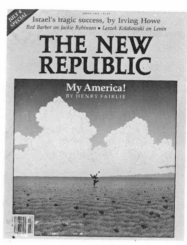

We felt liberated by Reagan's promise of a holy war.

Holy wars often begin with a child sacrifice, symbol of the coming sacrifice of the group's vitality. Reagan, too, spoke of child sacrifice. "The President," continued *The New Republic*, "was apocalyptic. He thrilled his audience with the tale of a man who said that 'I would rather see my little girls die now, still believing in God, than have them grow up under Communism . . .' "[11] Giving speeches about evil empires and dying children externalized Reagan's inner problems so well that reporters noticed that afterwards he looked radiant. "In the last few days," *The New York Times*' James Reston noted, "President Reagan and his wife have never seemed happier."[12] A *Daily News* reporter later said Reagan had "called life at the White house 'fulfilling,' adding: 'Some nights you go home feeling 10 feet tall.' "[13]

Reagan's promise of war affected every aspect of life in America. While domestic problems were almost completely neglected—the government borrowed $29.3 billion in May alone to meet its bills—a Congress which a few months earlier had turned down the first-strike MX missile now felt they "couldn't tie the President's hands" and approved it. "President Reagan looked wonderful the morning after the MX vote," reported *The Washington Post's* Mary McGrory. "His eyes were bright, his cheeks rosy . . . Not since the Gulf of Tonkin resolution has a president enjoyed such a triumph . . . The Democrats are buffaloed by Reagan's continuing, increasing hold on the country's affections."[14]

**We soared away from our inner problems on Reagan's
MX phallus.**

Similarly, after 20 years of turn-downs, Congress approved the B1
bomber, despite its immediate obsolescence and eventual $114 billion
price-tag.[15] Poison gas production was approved by Congress after a
14-year moratorium on production. The Navy stepped up its building
program, expanding from 400 to 700 ships. Creation of the new
100,000-man Rapid Deployment Force was hurried up, along with the
expansion of bases around the world stockpiled with tanks, helicopters,
artillery and ammunition. A 70 percent increase in the number of nuclear
warheads, from 25,000 to 42,000, was put into high gear, along with the
completion of hundreds of Cruise and Pershing 2 missiles to be placed
around Europe to carry out our mutual suicide pact.[16] In all, the largest
military buildup in the history of the world was being implemented,
amounting to a doubling of war expenditures during Reagan's first term.
What a cleansing a trillion dollars worth of destruction could give the
world!

The sexual excitement produced in us by so much phallic buildup was
reflected by our continuous use of the metaphor of fire, which so often
stands for sexual excitement in dreams. Central America, which had a
few months earlier been dubbed "a fire in our back yard," was now proclaimed by Reagan to be "a fire that is burning in our own front yard."
That we ourselves had created this sexual fire was obliquely admitted by
Reagan in one speech when he cited an earlier president as saying, "In
America, a glorious fire had been lighted upon the altar of liberty . . . let
the sparks that continually go up from it fall on other altars, and light up
in distant lands the fire of freedom." Central America would be our
sacrificial altar. We had transferred our sexual fire to them. Appropriately, we called the new CIA-*contra* base "Las Vegas," after the

Central America was "a fire in our front yard," a symbol of our sexual excitement.

sexual excitement of the gambling and prostitution facilities of that city. The more our economy revived, the more we saw this Central American fire as "out of control." Democrats in Congress held hearings in which they hallucinated that the situation was "deteriorating very rapidly" in Central America.[17] Republican Senator Barry Goldwater appeared on "Face the Nation" to declare that "If I were President . . . I would say . . . use our troops, our aircraft, our forces [to] quarantine Nicaragua and El Salvador [and] invade Cuba."[18] Those few critics who were

Cartoonists now regularly gave Reagan a gun to shoot someone.

puzzled as to why "a smoky nuisance fire had suddenly been declared out of control"[19] missed the sexual overtones of "the glorious fire" we saw burning so vividly in our "front yard" (our genitals).

Our military buildup in Central America began with the construction of military bases, airfields and radar installations in Honduras near the Nicaraguan and Salvadoran borders.[20] From these American camps, CIA-financed *contras* made terrorist sweeps into Nicaraguan villages and

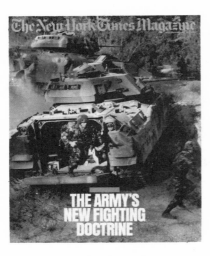

conducted bombings of Managua and other cities with CIA-owned planes, in an attempt to get Nicaragua to strike back.[21] All these activities were illegal, since it is against American law to help the overthrow of any government with which we were not at war. Yet what was regularly headlined as "Reagan's Secret War" didn't really need to be kept a secret. Polls at the time showed that "by 54 to 29 percent, citizens said Reagan is leading the United States toward war in Central America,"[22] while the public's approval of Reagan's handling of the presidency was rising to unprecedented levels. Obviously "leading the United States toward war in Central America" was what we approved of Reagan doing.

The army began preparing for war.

That most people also said, when asked directly, that they were "against war" only reflected their defensive level of motivations. What America wanted was *war without guilt*, and Reagan had promised us he could bring this about. It didn't even matter which side we backed. Polls showed only 8 percent knew which side we were on in the two countries.[23] What mattered was that we cheered Reagan on as he headed toward war.

Nor was it important that those we financed in El Salvador were led by a man described by former U.S. Ambassador Robert White as "a pathological killer" who helped torture and murder tens of thousands of innocent people, nor that we paid *contras* $1,000 a month to conduct bloody terrorist raids into Nicaragua to burn villages and shoot innocent women and children for target practice.[24] The President simply labeled the *contra* terrorists "freedom fighters," promised that "we're not going to lose a country to communism on our watch," put the Navy on a "war footing"[25] and continued to try to provoke a response.

Reagan's main problem was with Nicaragua. It is almost impossible to start a war with someone who refuses to play his role, and Nicaragua refused to respond to our provocations. It even stopped supplying arms to the Salvadoran rebels. At the same time that the Reagan administration was claiming to the American people that "The Communist world—Cuba, the Soviet Union, East Germany, Bulgaria—is pouring the stuff of war and propaganda into Central America,"[26] other U.S. officials were having to admit to Congress that "the flow of military supplies to Salvadoran rebels has been only a trickle for many months."[27] Since our financing of the *contras* was supposed to have been for "stopping the flow of arms," it was embarrassing to have Pentagon officials admit to the press that "they haven't confiscated any rifles or anything like that" with the tens of millions of dollars we furnished for that purpose.[28]

Yet psychologically we *had* to continue to imagine external threats. It couldn't just be all in our heads. We tried to play up individual incidents as much as we could. When one U.S. adviser was killed in El Salvador, *Newsweek* put him on the front cover with the hopeful headline "CENTRAL AMERICA: THE FIRST CASUALTY."[29] When two American journalists were blown up by a land mine in Honduras, the entire U.S. press corps reported—without evidence—that they had been killed by Nicaraguan artillery from across the border.[30] Yet a real incident continued to elude us.

We felt like bursting through to relieve our inner anxieties.

Reagan had to make a decision. All of his advisers were telling him that "he must 'win' Central America" if he wanted to run again.[31] But neither Nicaragua nor the Salvadoran rebels were cooperating. Should he nevertheless move militarily *without* a guilt-reducing *casus belli*? In a crucial National Security Council meeting on July 8, a task force reported to him that "the situation in Central America is nearing a critical point."[32] Reagan made his decision: move now.

In an action that was later described by a friendly reporter as "impulsive,"[33] Reagan ordered the sending of 5,000 American troops to Honduras to conduct "maneuvers" near the Nicaraguan border and the sending of a large naval battle armada to the coast of Nicaragua. The moves were delayed until the end of July, when Congress was about to adjourn.[34] Until then, he continued to say, "We are not doing anything to try and overthrow the Nicaraguan government."

At the end of July, Reagan, in a move "which took major congressional figures on both sides of the party by surprise,"[35] sent 5,000 troops

We wanted Reagan to show our muscle.

and a naval force of 19 ships, including a battleship, 2 aircraft carriers, 140 planes and 16,500 personnel to Central America. "The idea is to intimidate," a Pentagon official told *Time*.[36] Reagan's aides spoke of "a possible quarantine"—that is, an embargo, an act of war—around Nicaragua.[37] Under banner headlines reading "REAGAN GETS TOUGH ON CENTRAL AMERICA—U.S. BATTLE FLEET SAILS,"[38] the flotilla sailed south.

Would the American people approve of starting a war with no justification at all? Could they stand the guilt that would result? Various Reagan aides sent out "trial balloons" to the press to see how far we should go. U.N. Ambassador Jeane Kirkpatrick said "a demonstration of U.S. ability to interdict arms shipments on the high seas might be salutary."[39] U.S. Ambassador to Nicaragua Anthony Quainton said "the time is going to come" when the fleet would have to "quarantine Nicaragua."[40] Another official said "the presence of the flotilla of ships . . . could also serve for attack" in the region.[41] What would be the response by Americans to such suggestions?

As soon as it became clear that war without a guilt-reducing excuse was being contemplated, the media and the Congress gave the answer. "RISKING WAR FOR WHAT?" ran Tom Wicker's *New York Times* column.[42] "WEIGH IMPEACHMENT IN AN ILLEGAL WAR" ran

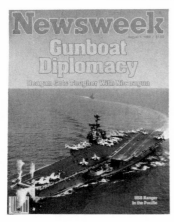

We tried to bring off our own Falklands victory.

another column.[43] "A FIRST STEP TO MORE GI GRAVES" read the front-page headline of the *Peoria Journal Star*. When the Congressman from Peoria showed this headline to Reagan, he told the President "we've got some work to do to get the American people on our side."[44] *The New York Times* asked "does the large United States naval battle group going into the area prefigure a quarantine or even a more extensive blockade? Does following through with force mean readiness to attack Soviet and Cuban ships and aircraft bound for Nicaragua, as in the 1962 Cuban missile crisis?"[45] "A blockade is an act of war," said one Congressman, "and the Constitution places the decision to go to war in the hands of Congress."[46] *The Washington Post* ran full-page interviews for the first time with Nicaraguan officials. One asked, "What wrong have we done to the people of the United States? Why does their government respond with a clenched fist?"[47] Nicaragua even agreed to discuss the issue of arms flow to El Salvador, despite lack of evidence that there was any, "because this supposedly is what most irritates the U.S. government."[48] Five thousand people marched in Washington to protest the military movements. Even though no major American newspaper was brave enough to report the march, the memory of Vietnam protests nevertheless remained potent. "The United States is being taken to war not only without a declaration from Congress but against its expressed desire," warned a *New York Times* editorial.[49] "Who will fight this war?" asked a Congressman during the House debate on the move.[50] "He thinks he's John Wayne," House Speaker Tip O'Neill was heard to mutter during the debate. "He thinks he can go down there and clear the place out."[51]

Obviously the guilt would be too great. Going to war without even a flimsy excuse would not be allowed.

When Reagan backed off, the let-down in mood was severe. The Right, the older psychoclass, was especially disappointed. Columnist Patrick Buchanan said Reagan was "impotent," proclaimed that "the Reagan Revolution is over, finished," and said that even if the Right didn't dump Reagan entirely, "the romance is forever gone out of the marriage."[52] A headline in one newsweekly called Washington "A City Without Guts."[53] For a few weeks Reagan's polls dropped precipitously.[54] Obviously something else would have to be tried. If the tentacles of the octopus couldn't be provoked into action, perhaps the head of the octopus could be.

Provocation of the enemy was the official task of the Air Force intelligence "Ferret" program. For many years the Air Force had been sending planes almost daily into Soviet territory to "tickle" their radar and defense systems in order to provoke responses such as the scrambling of fighters, the activation of radar and the firing of missiles. Despite the ever-present possibility that these "Ferret" provocations could start a nuclear war, American planes, according to *Time*, "had triggered the firings of more than 900 Soviet ground-to-air missiles, so far without a hit."[55] Over 25 aircraft had been attacked or

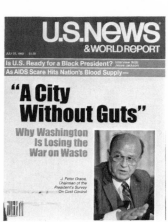

Washington was called "A City Without Guts" after Reagan backed off.

destroyed and more than 120 Americans killed in the past three decades by these secret and deadly games of provocation.[56]

The "Ferret" program included the use of commercial airliners to gather intelligence along Soviet borders. According to Ernest Volkman, National Security Editor for *Defense Science*, Korean Air Lines "regularly overflies Russian airspace to gather military intelligence."[57] KAL, says the *Boston Globe*, was essentially a military company, all of its pilots being military officers with high security clearance. U.S. army intelligence officials have admitted KAL commercial planes have in the past been equipped with side-view cameras and sent to border areas to take pictures.[59] One of these KAL commercial flights was the means used by American intelligence to provoke the enemy and give us our first sacrifice.

At the end of August, American intelligence learned that on September 1 the Soviet Union was going to test their new PL-5 missile on the Kamchatka Peninsula.[59] In order to learn all we could about the tests, we activated all our radar, infrared and radio listening posts in the area. These included the sophisticated "Cobra Dane" Air Force radar system on Shemya island at the end of the Aleutians, the "Cobra Judy" Navy ship radar system near Kamchatka, the U.S. spy satellite network, RC 135 spy planes with radar and other sensors and our regular radio monitoring posts in Japan and Alaska.[60]

Whether KAL 007 was purposely sent by the U.S. into Soviet territory as part of this intelligence gathering—either equipped with cameras and other sensors or as what the intelligence community refers to as "a target of opportunity"—is as yet not known. Most of the pertinent information has been locked up by a U.S. court as a part of a liability suite against KAL and the U.S. government brought by the families of those killed. The suit claims that the military "saw and recognized radar indications" that KAL 007 was in Soviet territory but deliberately took no action to warn the crew.[61]

U.S. intelligence watched KAL 007 fly into Soviet territory.

Whatever the reason for the flight's course deviation, all the details of the flight itself conform to a scenario of deliberate provocation of the Soviets by U.S. intelligence. As *The Washington Post Magazine* cover put it, "the U.S. watched" as the plane went into Soviet territory. Several crucial facts make this conclusion virtually inescapable:[62]

(1) KAL 007 was held up for 40 minutes past its scheduled takeoff time, coordinating its arrival time (3:00 A.M.) over the Kamchatka test site precisely with the moment the American "Ferret D" spy satellite was over the same site.

(2) The plane was equipped with several backup systems that made malfunctioning unlikely. But even if its computer was programmed incorrectly and then doublechecked carelessly, its weather radar system and compass would easily have shown the pilot he was off course and over land not ocean.

(3) The pilot, who had flown the route many times before, only had to look out the window to see the lights of the towns, roads and cars on Kamchatka to know he was not over the Pacific as he was supposed to be. Yet he continued to fly deeper into Soviet territory.

(4) The pilot remained in radio contact with both Tokyo air control and a second plane, KAL 015, flying behind it, so it would have been simple for U.S. intelligence to have warned it when it saw that the Soviets had discovered KAL 007, cancelled their missile test, scrambled its fighter planes and told its pilots to follow "the RC 135.

(5) U.S. intelligence could communicate directly to the President, the Secretary of Defense and the CIA, and could have put on their desks 10 minutes after transmission the information that KAL 007 was being chased by interceptors over Soviet territory. This would have given Reagan and his staff more than an hour and a half in the middle of a normal work day to warn the plane. Whether the President *was* told and then decided to allow the sacrifice or whether intelligence officers who were watching made the decision themselves is not now known.

Stories later ran in *The New York Times* and *The Washington Post Magazine* concluding that "United States intelligence experts say that they have reviewed all available evidence and found no indication that Soviet air defense personnel knew before the attack that the target was a commercial plane"[63] and that "the entire sweep of events—from the time the Soviets first began tracking KAL Flight 007 . . . to the time of the shootdown—was meticulously monitored and analyzed instantly by U.S. intelligence."[64] These revelations sank below national consciousness as though they had never been published. Every detail of the government version given to the public was later shown to have been incorrect. Though Reagan said, ''There is no way a pilot could mistake this for anything other than a civilian airliner,'' tapes later released showed pilots calling it ''an RC 135.'' Though the President said there was no warning by the Russians, the State Department later admitted tapes showed the pilot said, ''I am firing cannon bursts'' before firing the missile that knocked it down, and had even said the target ''does not respond to inquiries.''[65] The President's claim that the Russian pilot could easily see the plane's outline in the clear moonlight was contradicted by the State Department's later admission that the Russian plane was always 2,000 feet below the airliner and could not see an outline at all. When the Soviet plane fired its warning shots, KAL 007 gave no response and continued to head straight for Vladivostok on the Soviet mainland.[66] Since the Russians have always been paranoid about their borders, and since there was no way they could possibly know the plane wasn't carrying nuclear warheads, we could reliably count on them to shoot it down. What the President had called ''the Soviet massacre'' was in fact the first American sacrifice of the Reagan presidency.

We projected all our bloodlust into the Russian bear.

It felt good to have 269 sacrificial victims as proof that the enemy contained all our sadism. Reagan's popularity polls rose again. NBC-TV reported, "An administration official said this proves that all the bad things that Ronald Reagan had been saying about the Russians all these years were right."[67] Reagan himself—though he must have been fully aware that we had watched while the plane was heading for disaster and that the Russians had thought it was a military flight—called it "an act of barbarism." "This attack was not just against ourselves or the Republic of Korea," he told us. "This was the Soviet Union against the world." "SOVIET PARANOIA," screamed the *Orlando Sentinal*.[68] "MOSCOW'S BLOODY HANDS," said the *New York Post*.[69] The *Chicago Tribune* termed it "premeditated murder"[70] and *The New York Times* "cold-blooded mass murder."[71] "They are beasts equal to the Nazis," said New York's Mayor Koch.[72] While Americans burned Soviet flags at the U.N., newspapers reported that "REAGAN RIDES THE CREST OF AN ANTI-SOVIET WAVE" which had "defused the opposition to Administration policies in Central America" and had "assured the emplacement of new U.S. nuclear weapons in West Germany, Britain and Italy."[73] "Bloody as it was, the airlines shootdown was, for Reagan, a political bonus and a propaganda blessing," concluded the *Chicago Tribune*.[74] "It's going to make some things easier for us," a Presidential adviser said.[75] The President "couldn't have written a better script," a Democratic Senate aide said. "He [now] looks like *the president* . . . "[76]

There was just one problem. Reagan undoubtedly knew *consciously* that the "massacre" story was a lie. He couldn't therefore take immediate retaliatory action without stirring up too much of his own guilt.

The American people soon objected strongly to Reagan's lack of strong action. "The people of this country are beginning to question whether we have the moral strength . . . to take concerted action," said Senator D'Amato.[77] A Conservative movement spokesman put it more strongly: "The President has been talking like Superman, but his policies are more like those of Neville Chamberlain."[78] Polls showed Americans two to one saying Reagan was not tough enough on the Russians.[79] Cartoonists pictured him as a woman, hitting the Russian bear on the nose with a little slap of his purse. One right-wing columnist reported that "the President's oldest friends are alternately outraged and demoralized by the timidity of his response."[80] "This was Ronald Reagan's Falkland crisis," said Howard Phillips, Chairman of the Conservative Caucus, "and he did not respond appropriately."[81] Reagan was called by others "a windy wimp . . . a Wizard of Oz . . . a fake."[82]

Once again the American people had to taunt Reagan into more aggressive action. We even told him where to invade. "THE WAY TO ANSWER FLIGHT 007 OUTRAGE: GIVE MOSCOW HELL IN CENTRAL AMERICA," read a *New York Post* headline. But Central America was still being uncooperative. So Reagan turned first to two other sacrificial stages already in preparation—Beirut and Grenada.

9

KILLING THE POISONED
"The Wrath of Ron"

By the fall of 1983, the American economy was surging back to life. Fueled by the record borrowings of Reaganomics and by a 14 percent growth rate in the money supply, our Gross National Product was expanding at a brisk 8 percent rate, corporate profits were up 20 percent and the stock market was setting new records almost daily. "The euphoria just keeps building and building," said one stock broker. It was, he said, just like "a scene at a wild New Year's party."[1]

Yet—like the euphoria experienced at so many parties—the more the economy recovered, the worse we felt. Rather than being able to enjoy the fruits of our work, our Laser Eyes superego poisoned our pleasures as soon as we began to feel them. As a character in a current novel put it, "I can lose myself in work, but when it's over, there's that same hole inside. The problem is, we've seen that you come down from every high—sexual passion, drugs, meditation, political causes, money, work, achievement. Everything. It passes through you so quickly, like Chinese food."[2]

What could we do with our poisoned pleasures? We could dump them into sacrificial victims . . . then kill those who were full of our poison. Our delusional solution was identical to that of the Aztecs. They had ripped the poisoned heart out of their victims to cleanse their society of evil pleasures. Like the Aztecs, we believed that our soldiers could be containers for our poison. The more the economy boomed—the more sinful we felt—the more we imagined that we were pumping our soldiers full of our poison. The media that fall was dominated by two themes: the soaring economy and our military might. The two were linked in the unconscious. The message was: Now is the time to kill the poisoned.

So powerful was our need for a blood sacrifice, *The Washington Post* ran a full-page article on an exhibition featuring the art of Aztec human sacrifice which was being held by The National Gallery of Art. The article was dominated by a picture of a poisoned heart being ripped out from the victim's chest. Like a psychoanalytic patient's "free associations," the picture was an accurate glimpse into the depths of our unconscious group-fantasy. It was time for our sacrifice, too.

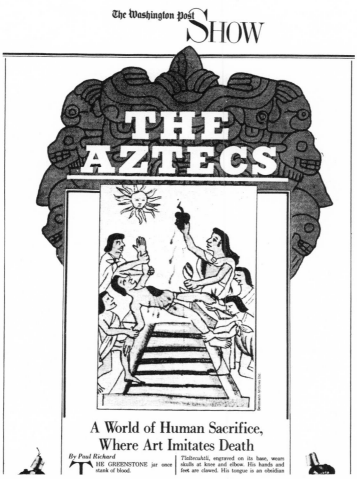

The Washington Post SHOW

THE AZTECS

A World of Human Sacrifice,
Where Art Imitates Death

By Paul Richard

THE GREENSTONE jar once stank of blood.

Tlaltecuhtli, engraved on its base, wears skulls at knee and elbow. His hands and feet are clawed. His tongue is an obsidian

A human sacrifice was pictured three weeks before the Beirut massacre.

For the past year, American marines in Beirut had been sitting behind the signs saying "Unload weapons before entering compound." Only a few had been killed so far. The problem was that the Syrians and others had trusted Reagan's statement that our troops would be fairly neutral and would be removed rather soon. To disabuse the Moslems of such a notion, President Reagan, on September 13, ordered that the Marines would for the first time use naval and air power against them, and we began bombarding Druse positions. "PREZ TAKES OFF GLOVES IN LEBANON," exulted the *New York Post*.[3] "We want to convince the Syrians that we will slap the shit out of them if they keep on trying to take over Lebanon," said a White House official.[4]

The Marines themselves felt relieved to be in real battle after waiting so long. As *The Miami Herald* reporter saw their response to their new role:

SOUND AND FURY:
MARINES RELISH TASTE OF BATTLE

The Marines may be in Lebanon as peacekeepers, but it's the fighting that gets their adrenalin going.

They loved it.

"At first, when we started taking rounds, it was a shock," said Lance Cpl. Jeff Becerril, 20, "but after two seconds we got in gear. It felt great."

"I hated to leave. It felt . . . good just to fire . . . We got off on it."[5]

Now Congress had to meet under the War Powers Act and approve of the military action. Reagan asked for faith in him. Congress gave it to him. It was their first official approval of the war trance. As one *Washington Post* columnist reported it, House Speaker Tip O'Neill, normally an opponent of Reagan's military policies, had inexplicably "passionately thrown himself behind Reagan on Lebanon in a way that left a number of representatives saddened. The speaker, highly emotional, repeatedly invoked the majesty of 'the president of the United States' (instead of saying 'Reagan' or 'the president,' as is usually the case.)"[6] The Congress approved 18 months for the sacrifice. It took only one month.

Congress approved the sacrifice.

The details had been carefully planned months in advance. According to the Department of Defense Commission Report which reconstructed the events leading up to the massacre, the Marines at the airport were given completely different instructions from those given to other Marines in Beirut on defending themselves. All the others were issued a "Blue Card" telling them to protect themselves from enemy fire according to usual Marine rules of engagement. The Marines at the airport, however, were given a "White Card" which told them that their weapons must be "not loaded" and instructed them that they were not "authorized to fire . . . on vehicles attempting unauthorized access" to their compound.[8] According to the Commission Report, this "White Card-Blue Card" system—which was explicitly approved several times by the entire chain of command, right up to the White House—was primarily responsible for the massacre. The Commission said there was a "mind-set" (their word for a group-fantasy) that irrationally led everyone to agree that the Marines at the airport should be more defenseless than the others. "The 'White Card-Blue Card' dichotomy," said the Commission, "tended to formalize that view. Interviews of individual Marines who performed duty at the two locations confirm this mind-set. In short, the Commission believes the Marines at BIA [Beirut International Airport] were conditioned by their ROE [White Card] to respond less aggressively to usual vehicular or pedestrian activity at their perimeter than were those Marines posted at the Embassy locations . . . Every Marine interviewed expressed concern over the restrictions against inserting magazines in weapons . . ."[9]

Thus everything that could be done to set up the sacrifice was now complete: (1) all 300 Marines at the airport were told to sleep in the same building, (2) signs were posted at the gates announcing that all weapons inside were unloaded, (3) gates were left open and without adequate barriers, (4) the sentries were forbidden to load their weapons, (5) the sentries were forbidden to open fire at unauthorized vehicles which tried to force their way in and (6) the Moslems were bombarded to let them know the Marines were now their enemy. In the week preceding the massacre, American intelligence received "strong and explicit warnings" that because of our stepped-up bombings of the Moslems there would be a "spectacular terrorist attack" on the Marines, but when this report was transmitted to Washington no action was taken to change the "White Card" rules of non-defense.[10] Although some National Security Council members urged Reagan "to pull back the U.S. Marines from Beirut to the U.S. fleet" because "the Lebanese Moslems viewed the U.S. Marines as an ally of the Christian militia which could be targeted," Reagan overruled them.[11] We had delegated to him the grim task of sacrificing those Marines, and he had promised us he would carry out our sacrifice. Five days before the massacre, Reagan phoned Thomas Dine, executive director of the

We all knew before the massacre that the Marines were "sitting ducks."

American-Israel Public Affairs Committee, to thank him for his help in getting the 18-month War Powers bill passed in Congress. Reagan told Dine that he had just talked to the parents of a Marine who had earlier been killed in Beirut. He then went on to say:

> You know, I turn back to your ancient prophets in the Old Testament and the signs foretelling Armageddon [the final conflict between good and evil], and I find myself wondering if—if we're the generation that is going to see that come about. I don't know if you've noted any of those prophecies lately, but, believe me, they certainly describe the times we're going through.[12]

Five days later, on October 23, 1983, a truck circled the Marine compound with its lights off, pulled up to the compound and the driver began taking pictures—which the guard thought "kind of strange." The driver cruised around again, then drove the truck through an iron gate left "invitingly" open and past two sentries with unloaded rifles.[13] By the time the sentries had loaded their weapons, the truck had run into the main building, detonating 12,000 pounds of explosives and killing 241 Marines. The second Reagan sacrifice was accomplished.

Reagan's response to the massacre was that it was "a horrifying reminder of the type of enemy that we face in many critical areas of the world today"—that is, it confirmed his paranoid conspiracy theories. The Marines, he said, "must stay there until the situation is under control." Most newspapers in America agreed with him.[14] Marine commandant General Paul Kelly said, "Thank God that this country of ours can still produce young Americans who are willing to lay down their life . . ."[15] Hordes of reporters invaded the homes of the Marines who had died, taking TV pictures of the delivery of death notices to the parents. "How did you feel when you heard your son was killed?" asked one.[16] Most parents said they felt proud; only a few said, "I feel my son was sacrificed," or, "I want someone to tell me why my son had to die."[17]

Two days later, more Marines were to die in Grenada. The invasion of the tiny island had been planned for six months, since right after President Reagan proclaimed that Grenada was the bearer of "the Communist virus" and showed us that fuzzy photo of their airfield on TV.[18] As *The Economist* summarized the advance planning:

> The CIA had long contemplated the overthrow of [Grenadan leader] Maurice Bishop but drew back after plans were leaked to congress. American marines even staged a mock invasion of "Amber and the Amerdines" near Puerto Rico in 1981. Bishop's fall on October 14th and the character of his successors naturally revived this enthusiasm. American officials in neighboring Barbados immediately discussed the question of "rescuing" Bishop . . .[19]

What happened after Bishop's fall on the 14th was widely reported to be that the murderous new leaders lined him up along with others before a wall at Fort Rupert and shot them. Only one reporter, Jeff Nesmith of *The Atlanta Journal and Constitution*, bothered to check this story out. What he found was that there was no blood at the spot of the supposed murders, that those who said they saw it, when re-questioned by him, admitted that they only had heard rumors of the shooting, that in fact the new leaders were "so anxious to avoid harming Bishop and a large crowd of his supporters that they had acceded to his demand that they disarm their men," and that Bishop most probably was "killed in a fluke in which an anti-tank grenade exploded in a room where they happened to be standing."[20]

The next ten days on what was to become known as "Terror Island" were similarly quiet. There was no fighting on the island, the beaches were crowded with sunbathers and the American medical students "were jogging as usual—curfew or no curfew."[21] On Sunday the 23rd, while a four-day curfew was still in effect, the American students held a meeting, and found that only 10 percent—mainly first semester students who had been there only six weeks—thought they might want to leave the island.[22] Although General Hudson Austin, the head of the new council, had promised to guarantee the students' safety, he said that when the curfew ended the next day those who wished to leave could do so. U.S. Embassy officials met on Sunday with Austin, the medical students and the University Chancellor, Dr. Geoffrey Bourne, who then told Washington that the "Americans in Grenada were not in danger . . ."[23] According to Bourne's son, "I received a call from a member of the board of trustees of the medical school . . . who said that the State Department was pressuring school officials in New York to say publicly that the students on Grenada were in danger so that Washington would have a pretext to invade the island."[24] The students' parents were so fearful that Reagan would use the students as "pretext hostages" that they sent a telegram, signed by over 500 parents, to the President asking him politely "not to move too quickly or to take any precipitous and provocative actions at this time."[25] The Chancellor even made a tape saying that the students were completely safe, and it was broadcast over Grenadan radio every 15 minutes to assure that the students' safety would not be used as a pretext for invasion.[26]

On Monday, the four-day curfew was lifted as promised, and the airport opened. Hedrick Smith of *The New York Times* later confirmed that there was "no difficulty leaving" and that "normal airport routines" were in operation, with "no armed guards" present—several flights, including his own, leaving peacefully.[27] The only flights which were cancelled were those of LIAT Airlines, and these had been cancelled not by the Grenadan government but by the U.S. and other Caribbean nations.[28] Representative Ronald Dellums, one of the Congressional delegates sent to Grenada on a fact-finding mission after the invasion, put the case succinctly:

*. . . The question of the students' safety was never the primary
concern* of either the policy-makers or the commanders of the
U.S. forces in their planning for this mission . . . In a 2½-hour
meeting that the congressional delegation had with the prime
ministers from the eastern Caribbean states, *the question of the
students' safety was never once raised.* Furthermore, our delegation *could not find one* confirmed instance in which an
American was threatened or endangered before the invasion. In
fact, the Grand Anse campus was a mere 20 meters from an unprotected beach. If the safety of the students was the primary
goal, why did it take the U.S. forces three days to reach it?[29]

We invaded a silent Terror Island.

On Tuesday morning, operation
Urgent Fury—what one American
diplomat called "the most
thoroughly planned crisis I've ever
participated in"—was unleashed.[30]
Citing our "overriding concern" for
"the safety of U.S. citizens,"[31]
America invaded the smallest nation
in the Western Hemisphere with
7,000 troops, 11 warships and
dozens of planes. Although it was
initially claimed that there were
"over 1,100 Cubans fighting to the
death," the number was later of-
ficially revised to "100
combatants."[32] Sunbathers and
joggers alike "watched in awe as
wave after wave of A-7 Corsair
fighters came out of the bright blue
sky, strafing with 20mm. cannons.
They were followed by slow-flying
AC-130s that unleashed deep death-
rattle groans as their electronic
Gatling guns lay down blankets of lead."[33] The hospital for the mentally
handicapped and children was bombed to rubble, killing at least 46.[34]
Unarmed Cuban construction workers, according to one eyewitness,
were "viciously gunned down in their dormitories."[35] Seven thousand
American troops pounded the island for four days to eliminate one hundred Cuban combatants. It was "one of the United States' finest hours,"
said one Senator. "We blew them away," said the commander of the
operation.[36] Over 8,000 medals were given out. We had successfully
"snapped the tentacle of the Russian octopus that threatened us."[37]

"We blew them away."

Official reasons for the invasion multiplied during the following week. The most effective with the American people was that the action was needed to save the students. Watching returning students kiss the ground and say they were "frightened to death by all the shooting" allowed us the illusion that it was shooting *before* the invasion, not after it, that they were talking about.[38] The second official reason was that "a Cuban occupation of the island had been planned" and that "we got there just in time" to prevent it.[39] The evidence for this was said to be based on "documents, some of which the officials said would be made public after they had been translated and analyzed [which] shows that Cuba planned to send hundreds of troops to Grenada within the next several weeks" and that "serious consideration was being given to seizing Americans as hostages . . ."[41] The Pentagon later had to sheepishly admit that this was a mistranslation of the captured documents, and that there was no mention of any Cuban troops arriving.[42] The third official reason—"to restore democracy"—was made dubious two weeks later when the new leader whom we installed, Paul Scoon, banned public meetings, authorized arrests without warrants, set up press censorship and indefinitely postponed elections.[43]

The actual motives behind the invasion lay in the unconscious dynamics of the war trance. Grenada was a "hot spot," a place to dump our poisoned sexuality and vitality, a place to rape-and-kill. Just as we went into Vietnam "to prevent Moscow from having an orgasm," so, too, we invaded Grenada "to prevent Moscow from feeling potent." As a Reagan aide who was present at the meetings in which the decision to invade was made recalled it:

> The purpose was to deny the Russians/Cubans a feeling of potency in grabbing small vulnerable states in the region.[44]

Much of the imagery used during the invasion paralleled this "deny the Russians a feeling of potency" theme of preventing forbidden excitement—from press secretary Larry Speakes' statement that Grenada was "a floating crap game" which we had to end to the more open language of the Marine who, when asked why he had to invade, said: "I want to fuck communism out of this little island, and fuck it right back to Moscow."[45]

That our rape-and-kill fantasy required several hundred real dead bodies was not just an unfortunate byproduct of the invasion but the most important part of the cleansing power of the sacrifice.[46] The whole nation watched on TV as the caskets paraded by the reviewing stand. While everyone stood stiff, President Reagan assured us that the dead need not be prayed for "because they are safe in God's loving arms."[47]

We sent our Marines to "God's loving arms," carrying our sins.

Only one person watching the parade did not enter into the war trance: the little boy of one of the dead Marines, who could be heard to ask his mother, "Where's my daddy?"

America was exultant over the invasion. It was called "Ronald Reagan's 'Falkland Islands' victory' " and "the most popular invasion since E.T."[48] Americans everywhere expressed their feelings of relief that Reagan had finally acted: "Thank God, we finally have a real man in the White House";[49] "U.S. soldiers' boot prints on Grenada's soil have done more than the MX will do to make U.S. power credible";[50] "Reagan is the first American President to recapture for the West a colony of the Soviet empire."[51] The American people, Congress and the media were overwhelmingly in favor of the invasion.[52] When Congressman Ted Weiss said on "Night Line" that he was about to introduce a resolution impeaching Reagan for unconstitutionally unilaterally declaring war by invading, host Ted Koppel said, "But . . . but . . . our polls show 9 to 1 in favor of it!"[53] After Reagan gave his October 28th address to the nation praising the Marines who died in Beirut and Grenada for their "courageous sacrifice," his polls went up 11 points and Marine recruiting officials were flooded with thousands of young men, many saying "I want to die for my country."[54] The third Reagan sacrifice was definitely a success, one we hoped to repeat. As one commentator put it, "Grenada was a lovely war, such a smash hit at the box office they're talking about a sequel."[55]

For although the cleansing action of the Grenadan invasion would enable us to delay starting a larger war for a while, there was little doubt in anyone's mind that it also both legitimated and authorized Reagan's use of military force to make us feel good. As a *Washington Post* reporter wrote right after the invasion was over:

"WHERE ELSE CAN WE SEND THEM?"

We planned a sequel to Grenada.

3 DAYS TURNED THE TALK OF 3 YEARS INTO ACTIONS

Suddenly, U.S. paratroopers were landing on a tiny Caribbean island, and body bags were coming back from Lebanon and Grenada.

Enlistments rose at U.S. Marine Corps recruiting stations while a string of televised ceremonies observed the return of almost 260 coffins. Patriotic rhetoric flowed from some while public-opinion polls showed fear of war increasing under President Reagan even as his popularity climbed.

In many ways, the contrasts mirrored the notion that something important, yet bewildering, was happening. Within three October days, three years of hard-line administration rhetoric seemed finally to have been transformed into action.

Almost a decade after the Vietnam war ended, the use of military power, and along with it a degree of risk and uncertainty, had been reintroduced into U.S. foreign policy . . .[56]

The first three Reagan sacrifices authorized more sacrifice even as they confirmed the conspiratorial view that *the same people did them all.* As one Reagan official put it, "Grenada, Beirut and the K.A.L. airliner all served to confirm in the President's mind his own view of the world, that there was a common thread to all these events and it all led back to Moscow."[57] That the common thread led inside us, not outside us, was clearly impossible to admit. Since so few Americans had been killed, we had to have a fourth sacrifice to finally cleanse the world of our sins. As one senior administration official put it in the wake of the invasion, "If the question is 'Could we again use military force responsibly as we did in Grenada?' the clear answer would be 'yes.' "[58]

After the invasion, it felt wonderful to have completely externalized all our emotional problems. Pollsters were startled to discover in the following months that Reagan's approval ratings stayed at all-time heights. As George Gallup put it, "Such a strong approval trend on the part of an incumbent president seeking re-election is without precedent in Gallup's 50 years of polling experience."[59] "America's days of weakness are over," Reagan promised us, praising the spirit of "sacrifice" on the part of our soldiers and telling us stories of airplane pilots who had chosen to go down with their planes rather than use their parachutes.[60] The whole country felt the excitement of the war trance. "There is something in the air, something vital and vibrant, strong," said Vice President Bush.[61] Immediately following Reagan's triumphant announcement of his re-election plans, WNBC-TV switched to a "man-in-the-street" for his reaction. He responded with a grin: "We've got to go out and fight someone." "CLAMOR GROWS FOR REPLAY OF GRENADA IN NICARAGUA," headlined *The Chicago Tribune,* while "Saturday Night Live" invited its listeners to send in their choice of nations to invade next.[62] Reagan's promise to give us another Grenada would surely be enough to re-elect him for another four years of joyful triumph.

Reagan rejoiced over Grenada.

So powerful was the manic feeling of excitement after Grenada, all of America seemed to have acquired an erection as we awaited the next rape-and-kill invasion. "Americans are now standing tall and firm," Reagan told us, and columnists echoed his metaphor by praising him for "stiffening our foreign policy."[63] Rape stories acquired new prominence in the news media, from specials discussing rape to fictional portrayals of rape victims. The media covered in great detail the career of Christopher Wilder, who raped and killed young women all across the country, and we watched night after night on TV the trial of six men in New Bedford, Massachusetts who had been accused of raping a woman on a barroom

We seemed to have an erection while we awaited the next exciting invasion.

pool table while others cheered them on. No one was surprised when, after the conviction, crowds demonstrated in favor of the convicted men—it was all part of our new fascination and identification with rapists. As one addict of the trial told *The Boston Globe*, "We don't get cable here, but that's O.K. because this show has a rape victim too. Rape must be 'in' this year."[64]

Besides rape, cannibalistic fantasies multiplied in the media—representing our "biting" rage, just like the "Man-Eater" fantasies of primitive ritual. Usually we experienced our biting rage only in projected form. While our top song warned us

We were so angry, we felt like biting someone.

"Watch out boys, she'll chew you up—She's a Man Eater" and our Democratic candidates for president asked "Where's the beef?", our president told us that, "like a roving wolf, Castro's Cuba looks to peace-loving neighbors with hungry eyes and sharp teeth."[65] Sometimes our cannibalistic wishes came close to breaking through into consciousness in their most regressed form—that of eating babies—as we made jokes on national TV about how much fun it would be to hack up, boil and eat Cabbage Patch dolls, which children that Christmas had taken to "adopting" by the millions in an intuitive attempt to forestall our infanticidal wishes toward them. Like Frosch's paranoid patient, we had come to see the whole world as full of our angry, biting teeth, and we needed a tough, angry leader who could "bite first" before we ourselves were devoured.[67]

We wanted Reagan to be tough and fight a world full of our own biting teeth.

By the beginning of 1984, that world was so full of our own biting anger that Reagan's America finally reached a totally delusional state of group-fantasy. Although actual terrorist activity in America was decreasing in frequency,[68] a wall of concrete antitank barricades and ground-to-air missiles was put around the White House for the first time in our history. "The fear in Washington is as puzzling as it is palpable," said *Newsweek*,[69] while Senator Moynihan predicted, "I think the prospect of 1984 being the year they bring the war to our shores is real."[70]

Because we were threatened by our own anger everywhere, we had to take the offensive everywhere—at home, as our factories poured out deadly weapons at a rate far exceeding that of any former war; in Europe, as we deployed our new missiles; in Korea, with a 200,000-troop "Team Spirit 84" exercise; around the world, with a 150,000-man Strategic Air Command "Global Shield 84" exercise; in space with our new "Star Wars" program. Unless we kept on the attack, we would be "defeated," and this would have a "poisonous impact" on the world.[71] As one columnist put it, "Yesterday it was Grenada that provided the

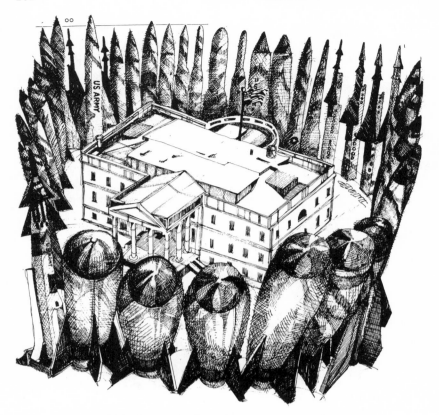

By 1984, Reagan's America was an armed camp.

pretext for poison. Tomorrow it could be Nicaragua.''[72] We *had* to attack our sinful poisons abroad, or they would return to poison us at home. In the extremities of our psychotic thinking, mining Nicaraguan ports and bombing Salvadoran peasants and financing *contra* terrorists and conducting 30,000-man ''exercises'' in Central America were acts of a country which feels itself to be under seige, necessary to prevent us from being engulfed by the delusional poison around us. As Reagan had told us so often, mere defensive action was now no longer enough. America had to take the offensive. ''We do not seek a military stalemate,'' he said. ''We seek victory.''[73]

The hardest part would be finding a *casus belli* for our final offensive against evil. Those who, like columnist William F. Buckley, Jr., suggested that Reagan should ''ask Congress for a declaration of war against Nicaragua''[74] were not taking into account that this would make most of us feel too guilty. We would need to engineer some humiliating incident which would prove the inhumanity of "the enemy" and "leave us no choice" but to fight. We seemed confident we could find this inci-

"Super Tuesday, huh? Y'call *that* a showdown?"

We knew Reagan would soon use the guns we had given him.

dent. As Secretary of State George Schultz said upon returning from Nicaragua, "They'd damn well better worry about the survival of their regime."[75] The final cleansing sacrifice of Reagan's America would not be long in coming.

REFERENCES

The research upon which this book is based was the Fantasy Analysis of 110 periodicals conducted over the past four years at The Institute for Psychohistory. I would like to express my thanks to the Research Associates of the Institute—particularly to Casper Schmidt, M.D., without whose help this book would not have been written—and to Jerome B. Rosen, Rudolph Binion, Susan Hein and Neil deMause for their invaluable aid in the preparation of this book.

A discussion of the concepts used in this book may be found in Lloyd deMause, *Foundations of Psychohistory*. New York: Creative Roots, 1982. Further studies describing the psychohistorical techniques used herein can be found in the journals of the Institute for Psychohistory, *The Journal of Psychohistory* and *The Journal of Psychoanalytic Anthropology*, the books of The Psychohistory Press and the Bulletin and Newsletter of the International Psychohistorical Association. Literature describing these publications may be obtained by writing The Institute for Psychohistory, 2315 Broadway, New York, New York 10024.

Unless otherwise indicated, all quotations from President Ronald Reagan are taken from the *Weekly Transcript of Presidential Documents* and all economic figures from Commerce Department publications.

1. THE SHOOTING OF RONALD REAGAN
"The King Must Die"

1. As the chart below shows, Federal debt as a percentage of GNP was at an all-time low since the 1930s (bottom line). It was actually *private* debt which was at an all-time high. Our guilt at the increase in our private debt was projected onto the Federal government, and the media invented a "soaring" Federal debt to condemn.

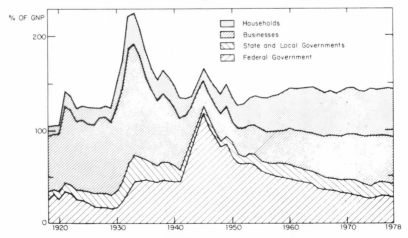

Outstanding debt of U.S. nonfinancial borrowers.

2. Commerce Department figures show corporate investment in 1980 at 11.3% of GNP, compared with 10.5% in 1970 and 9.6% in 1960. This is not to deny that the U.S. could have benefited from higher corporate investment (most industrial countries saved double the U.S. rate of 6% of income)—only that U.S. investment was increasing, not dropping, during the previous two decades.

3. The consensus of economic opinion attributed something over half of the decline in inflation during 1981 to factors which had nothing to do with Reagan's fiscal policies.

4. Poll cited in Adam Smith, "Your Next Leader Is Behind You." *Esquire*, October, 1982, p. 23.

5. For a full empirical study of the four stages of group-fantasy, see Lloyd deMause, *Foundations of Psychohistory*. New York: Creative Roots, 1982.

6. November 2, 1980, p. 28. The technical rules for Fantasy Analysis are explained in deMause, *Foundations*, pp. 194ff.

7. Government expenditures on goods and services as a percentage of GNP from 1975 to 1980 were: 22.1, 21.2, 20.9, 20.5, 20.1 and 20.3.

8. Flora Lewis, *N.Y. Times*, March 9, 1981, p. 29.

9. *Newsweek*, February 16, 1981, p. 20.

10. *Time*, March 2, 1981, cover.

11. *N.Y. Post*, February 6, 1981, p. 1.

12. *Kansas City Star*, March 29, 1981, p. 38A.

13. *Newsweek*, February 23, 1981, p. 18.

14. Ibid, p. 19.

15. Ibid.

16. *Des Moines Sunday Register*, March 29, 1981, p. 1.

17. *N.Y. Times*, March 13, 1981, p. 1.

18. James Fallows, "The Great Defense Deception." *N.Y. Review of Books,* May 28, 1981, pp. 15-19.

19. *U.S. News & World Report*, March 9, 1981, p. 18.

20. *Harper's*, December, 1980, p. 41.

21. *N.Y. Times Magazine*, March 15, 1981, p. 45.

22. *New Republic*, November 8, 1980, p. 18.

23. *N.Y. Times*, January 15, 1981, p. C2.

24. *Time*, February 23, 1981, p. 12.

25. Ibid.

26. For an excellent discussion of the literature on the killing of the new king in ritual combat, see Robert Paul, *The Tibetan Symbolic World: Psychoanalytic Explorations*. Chicago: University of Chicago Press, 1982, pp. 13ff.

27. Anthony Lewis, *N.Y. Times*, January 11, 1981, p. E23.

28. The best popular account of these studies can be found in Frank Browning, "Nobody's Soft on Crime Anymore," *Mother Jones*, August, 1982, pp. 25-31.
29. As only one instance, the *L.A. Times* on March 29, the day before the shooting of Reagan, featured a large picture on the first page of a gunshot victim being treated in a medical center, plus a major story on "the current quality of trauma care"—a story which at other times would have been accorded inside-page treatment.
30. For evidence of Institute for Psychohistory forecast of shooting of Reagan, see Robert Finen, "Two Student Views," *Journal of Psychohistory* 11 (1983): 113-114.
31. Aaron Latham, "The Dark Side of the American Dream," *Rolling Stone*, August 5, 1982, pp. 18ff.
32. Ibid, p. 54. Hinckley said he got the "signal" from a newspaper list of Reagan's schedule for the day; since this schedule was actually printed every day, it is more probable that his feeling was accurate that he had picked up the signal from the media, but that he was actually picking it up from the *total* media content during that week before the shooting.
33. *N.Y. Post,* April 1, 1981, p. 41; *Kansas City Star*, April 19, 1981, p. 33.
34. Author's poll, taken during the week following the shooting, of 230 college students in three colleges in New York and New Jersey, about one-third of whom were adults in night school and the rest undergraduate-age students.
35. *N.Y. Post*, April 6, 1981, p. 29.
36. *Des Moines Register,* April 12, 1981, p. C1.
37. *Time*, April 27, 1981, p. 16.
38. *N.Y. Times*, April 29, 1981, p. A22.
39. *N.Y. Post*, April 29, 1981, p. 2.

2. CREATING THE IRANIAN CRISIS
"Slipping Toward Impotence"

1. My analysis draws upon John J. Hartman, "Carter and the Utopian Group-Fantasy," in Lloyd deMause and Henry Ebel, eds., *Jimmy Carter and American Fantasy*. New York: Psychohistory Press, 1977, pp. 97-116.
2. For Hartman's analysis of why utopian wishes are defenses against threats of group decay and dissolution, see ibid, p. 113, and references to literature therein.
3. For a more complete Fantasy Analysis of the Carter period, see deMause, *Foundations*, pp. 221-230.

4. *New Republic*, April 29, 1978, p. 5.
5. *Time*, April 30, 1979, p. 18.
6. *N.Y. Times*, October 10, 1977, p. 1.
7. *N.Y. Times*, October 16, 1977, p. 30.
8. Vermont Royster, *Wall Street Journal*, March 1, 1978.
9. The figure is that of real Gross National Product per capita, that is, U.S. goods and services corrected for inflationary changes and changes in population, from 1948 to 1978.
10. *The Guardian*, June 25, 1978, p. 17.
11. As reported by TRB in *New Republic*, February 17, 1979, p. 37 and March 10, 1980, p. 3.
12. *N.Y. Times*, August 7, 1979, p. A15.
13. John Osborn, *New Republic*, August 4, 1979, p. 13.
14. *N.Y. Post*, July 23, 1979, p. 1.
15. *N.Y. Times*, September 2, 1979, p. E15.
16. For a description of the psychic mechanism of projective identification, whereby one puts one's craziest feelings into another person for safekeeping, see Thomas H. Ogden, *Projective Identification and Psychotherapeutic Technique.* New York: Jason Aronson, 1982.
17. Max Lerner, *N.Y. Post*, February 12, 1979; James Wechsler, *N.Y. Post,* February 22, 1979, p. 23.
18. *Village Voice*, March 26, 1979, p. 1.
19. *Time*, March 17, 1980, p. 17.
20. See Lloyd deMause and Henry Ebel, eds., *Jimmy Carter and American Fantasy.* New York: Psychohistory Press, 1977; Lloyd deMause, "Historical Group-Fantasies," *The Journal of Psychohistory* 7(1979):1-70 (reprinted in deMause, *Foundations*); public speeches by deMause at Institute for Psychohistory and at 1977 and 1978 Conventions of the International Psychohistorical Association; and six radio interviews on WOR and WBAI during those years. For a description of the response by the press and by academics to these predictions, see Chapter 7 of *Foundations.*
21. *N.Y. Times*, June 29, 1979, p. 1.
22. Jimmy Carter, *Keeping Faith: Memoirs of a President.* New York: Bantam Books, 1982, pp. 118-19.
23. *N.Y. Post*, July 11, 1979, p. 21.
24. Ibid.
25. For a psychological explanation of the roots of blood sacrifice, see deMause, *Foundations,* chapter 7.
26. The Gallup Poll of May, 1978 reported 53.4% of adult Americans had had a lasting born-again Christian religious experience. For the sacrificial core of Christianity and its connections with human sacrifice, see Hyam Maccoby, *The Sacred Executioner: Human Sacrifice and the Legacy of Guilt.* New York: Thames and Hudson,

1982. Also see sections on sacrifice in deMause, *Foundations,* Chapter 7.

27. For a brilliant analysis of the process of setting the sacrificial stage, see Casper G. Schmidt, "The Use of the Gallup Poll as a Psychohistorical Tool." *The Journal of Psychohistory* 10(1982). I have followed Schmidt in all the references to the Gallup Poll in this book.

28. See full references to these events in deMause, *Foundations*, pp. 304-5.

29. *Newsweek*, June 11, 1979, p. 71.

30. For a full theoretical and empirical description of this process of deflecting rage from the leader to an outside "enemy," see deMause, *Foundations,* Chapters 5-7.

31. Ralph G. Martin, *A Hero for Our Time.* N.Y.: Macmillan, 1983.

32. Terence Smith, "Why Carter Admitted the Shah," *N.Y. Times Magazine*, May 28, 1981, p. 37; Document reportedly obtained by Rep. George Hansen, for which see *N.Y. Post* report, November 28, 1979, p. 2.

33. Jimmy Carter, *Keeping Faith*, p. 455.

34. The Carter quote can be found in three substantively similar versions: *N.Y. Times*, November 18, 1979, p. 1; *Newsweek*, November 19, 1979, p. 68; and Carter, *Keeping Faith*, p. 455.

35. The full story of the lie can be seen clearly in Terence Smith, "Why Carter Admitted the Shah," *N.Y. Times Magazine*, May 28, 1981, p. 36; Lawrence K. Altman, "The Shah's Health: A Political Gamble," *N.Y. Times Magazine*, May 28, 1981, p. 50; Roy A. Chilas, Jr., "The Iranian Drama," *The Libertarian Review,* February, 1980, pp. 26-37; Hamilton Jordan, *Crisis: The Last Year of the Carter Presidency.* New York: G. P. Putnam's Sons, 1982, p. 31; and Michael Ledeen and William Lewis, *Debacle: The American Failure in Iran.* New York: Alfred Knopf, 1981, p. 220. Dr. Kean's suit against the journal *Science* also confirmed his giving of advice that the Shah could have been treated in Mexico; see *N.Y. Times*, May 26, 1981, p. C2. Only Terence Smith, in the article cited at the beginning of this reference, wondered why 'One option that, curiously, was never seriously examined was the evacuation of embassy personnel prior to admitting the Shah.''

36. The switch in mood is examined in Betty Glad, *Jimmy Carter: In Search of the Great White House.* New York: W. W. Norton, 1981, p. 468; quote from *New Yorker*, December 24, 1979, p. 27.

37. DeMause, *Foundations*, p. 307.

38. *N.Y. Post,* November 9, 1979, p. 2, November 12, 1979, p. 3 and December 4, 1979, p. 3; Carter quote from Hamilton Jordan, *Crisis,* p. 55.

39. *N.Y. Times*, November 25, 1979, p. 16.

40. James Brady, *N.Y. Post*, December 17, 1979, p. 26.
41. *Newsweek*, July 12, 1982, p. 16; *N.Y. Times Magazine*, April 18, 1982, p. 28.
42. *N.Y. Daily News,* January 19, 1980, p. 1.
43. William F. Buckley, Jr., *N.Y. Post*, March 11, 1980, p. 23.
44. *N.Y. Post*, February 2, 1980, p. 18.
45. *N.Y. Times,* January 30, 1980, p. A18.
46. *Time*, January 14, 1980, p. 32.
47. *N.Y. Post*, December 15, 1979, p. 7.
48. *New Republic,* March 15, 1980, p. 12.
49. *Village Voice*, February 25, 1980, p. 16; *N.Y. Post*, January 8, 1980, p. 3; *Time*, April 21, 1980, p. 14; *New Yorker*, April 28, 1980, p. 33; *N.Y. Times*, April 13, 1980, p. 1E.
50. *Newsweek,* July 12, 1980, p. 16; Drew Middleton, "Going the Military Route," *N.Y. Times Magazine,* May 28, 1981, p. 103.
51. *N.Y. Times*, May 15, 1980, p. 1; *N.Y. Times*, April 18, 1980, p. 1.
52. *N.Y. Post*, April 9, 1980, p. 1.
53. Andrew Young, "Penthouse Interview," *Penthouse*, February, 1983, p. 142.
54. Richard Nixon, on the Barbara Walters Special, ABC-TV, June 10, 1980.
55. Russell Baker, *N.Y. Times*, May 3, 1980, p. 23, described accurately what it felt like to be "choking" on a "bone in the throat" from our own "powerlessness."

3. THE MAKING OF A FEARFUL LEADER
"Where's the Rest of Me?"

1. Ronald Reagan, *Where's the Rest of Me?* New York: Karz Publishers, 1981 (1965), pp. 4-6.
2. For a brilliant psychohistorical analysis of the theme of punishment for sexual desires in *King's Row* and its connection with Reagan's personality, see Michael Rogin, "Ronald Reagan: Where's the Rest of Him." *Democracy,* April, 1981, pp. 33-38 and Michael Rogin, "Ronald Reagan's American Gothic." *Democracy*, October, 1981, pp. 51-59.
3. Lou Cannon, *Reagan*. New York: G. P. Putnam's Sons, 1982, p. 226; *RWR: The Official Ronald Wilson Reagan Quote Book*. St. Louis: Chain-Pinkham Books, 1980, p. 11.
4. Reagan's supposed "difficulty" in drawing extremities is belied by some of his doodles where they are quite competently drawn; for examples and references, see Kathy Randall Davis, *But What's He Really Like?* Menlo Park, California: Pacific Coast Publishers,

1970, p. 94; *U.S. News & World Report,* July 6, 1981, p. 19; *New York Post,* March 28, 1981, p. 25.

5. Bill Boyarsky, *The Rise of Ronald Reagan.* New York: Random House, 1968, p. 196.

6. Lou Cannon, *Ronnie and Jessie: A Political Odyssey.* New York: Doubleday and Co., 1969, p. 177.

7. Ibid.

8. Cannon, *Reagan,* p. 25.

9. Reagan, *Where's the Rest of Me?,* pp. 7-9.

10. Frank van der Linden, *The Real Reagan.*New York: William Morrow and Co., 1981, pp. 30 and 52.

11. Reagan, *Where's the Rest of Me?,* pp. 9 and 11.

12. For a general survey of the evolution of childrearing, see Lloyd deMause, Editor, *The History of Childhood.* New York: Psychohistory Press, 1974; for more detailed analysis on American childrearing during Reagan's childhood, see Glenn Davis, *Childhood and History in America.* New York: Psychohistory Press, 1976.

13. Van der Linden, *The Real Reagan,* p. 38.

14. Reagan, *Where's the Rest of Me?,* p. 16.

15. Reagan to Mark Shields, "President Reagan's Wide World of Sports." *Inside Sports,* March 31, 1981, p. 26.

16. Van der Linden, *The Real Reagan,* pp. 31 and 74.

17. Ibid, p. 73.

18. Cannon, *Reagan,* p. 93.

19. Charles D. Hobbs, *Ronald Reagan's Call to Action.* Nashville: Thomas Nelson, 1976, p. 23.

20. For a description of the dynamics of phobic fears, see Leon Salzman, *Treatment of the Obsessive Personality.* New York: Jason Aronson, 1980, pp. 105-121.

21. Sigmund Freud, "The Interpretation of Dreams," *Standard Edition,* 4, p. 260.

22. Obituary in *The New York Times,* May 19, 1941, p. 17.

23. Laurence Leamer, "The Great Pretenders," *California Magazine,* April, 1983, p. 154.

24. Van der Linden, *The Real Reagan,* p. 621.

25. Bill Boyarsky, *Ronald Reagan: His Life & Rise to the Presidency.* New York: Random House, 1981, pp. 29 and 49.

26. Reagan, *Where's the Rest of Me?,* p. 195.

27. Cannon, *Reagan,* p. 30.

28. Reagan, *Where's the Rest of Me?,* p. 195.

29. For a description of the mechanism of injecting wishes into others for purposes of control, see Thomas H. Ogden, *Projective Iden-*

tification and Psychotherapeutic Technique. New York: Jason Aronson, 1982.

30. Reagan, *Where's the Rest of Me?,* pp. 6-7.
31. Cannon, *Reagan,* p. 90.
32. F. Clifton White and William J. Gill, *Why Reagan Won.* New York: Regnery Gateway, 1981, p. 23.
33. Cannon, *Reagan,* p. 148.
34. Boyarsky, *Ronald Reagan,* p. 140.
35. Van der Linden, *The Real Reagan,* p. 82.
36. Boyarsky, *The Rise of Ronald Reagan,* p. 23.
37. George H. Smith, *Who Is Ronald Reagan?* New York: Pyramid Books, 1968, p. 115.
38. *The Wall Street Journal,* August 1, 1980, p. 32.
39. Edmund G. Brown and Bill Brown, *Reagan: The Political Chameleon.* New York: Praeger Publishers, 1976, pp. 46 and 123.
40. Ibid.
41. Smith, *Who Is Ronald Reagan?,* p. 95.
42. Ibid, p. 124.
43. Van der Linden, *The Real Reagan,* p. 91.
44. Hedrick Smith, Adam Clymer, Leonard Silk, Robert Lindsey and Richard Burt, *Reagan the Man, the President.* New York: Macmillan Publishing Co., 1980, p. 47.
45. Cited in Robert Scheer, "The Reagan Question," *Playboy,* August, 1980, p. 248.
46. Cannon, *Reagan,* p. 152.
47. Otto Fenichel, *The Psychoanalytic Theory of Neurosis.* New York: W. W. Norton & Co., 1945, pp. 211-212.
48. For a thorough discussion regarding the lawfulness of wars, including the seeming exception to the rule about wars not occurring during the first year of the presidency, the American Civil War, see deMause, *Foundations,* Chapters 5-7.
49. Ibid, p. 160.
50. Ibid, pp. 155-157.
51. Ibid, p. 211.
52. For detailed descriptions of Johnson's need to persecute others for his own disavowed traits, see Robert A. Caro, *The Years of Lyndon Johnson: The Path to Power.* New York: Alfred A. Knopf, 1982, and Doris Kearnes, *Lyndon Johnson & the American Dream.* New York: Harper & Row, 1976. Psychohistorical study has not yet begun on Truman.
53. John Deardourff to Martin Smith, "Reagan's Latest Campaign Brings Same Message, But New Audience." *Sacramento Bee,* November 18, 1979.

54. For an analysis of the various polls after the debate, see Cannon, *Reagan,* p. 298.
55. *Newsweek,* November 29, 1982, p. 44.
56. For a history of Reagan's advocacy of military force as a response to dozens of past political events abroad, see Murray N. Rothbard, "The Two Faces of Ronald Reagan." *Inquiry,* July 7, 1980, pp. 16-19.

4. REAGANOMICS AS A SACRIFICIAL RITUAL
"Cut, Slash, Chop"

1. Alvin H. Hansen, *Fiscal Policy and Business Cycles.* New York: Norton, 1941, pp. 18-24.
2. Maurice N. Walsh, ed., *War and the Human Race.* New York: Elsevier, 1971, p. 78.
3. Paul A. Samuelson, *Economics.* Eleventh Edition. New York: McGraw-Hill Book Co., 1980, p. 244.
4. Robert E. Lucas, Jr., *Studies in Business-Cycle Theory.* Cambridge, Mass.: MIT Press, 1981, p. 226.
5. For the psychogenic theory of the basis of technological progress in the evolution of childrearing, see deMause, *Foundations,* Chapter 4. The comparative study of primitive economics centers on the work of Karl Polanyi and his associates; see George Dalton, ed. *Primitive, Archaic and Modern Economics: Essays of Karl Polanyi.* Comparative anthropological study of primitive economics began in earnest with the work of M J. Herkovits; see his *Economic Anthropology.* New York: Alfred A. Knopf, 1952.
6. See deMause, *Foundations,* pp. 16 and 274 and deMause, "Comments on Lloyd deMause's 'Fetal Origins of History,'" *The Journal of Psychoanalytic Anthropology* 5(1982): 483-4.
7. See, for instance, Theodore H. Gaster, *Thespis: Ritual, Myth and Drama in the Ancient Near East.* New York: Harper & Row, n.d.
8. The description given here of the ritual cycles of the Kwakiutl is taken from Irving Goldman, *The Mouth of Heaven: An Introduction to Kwakiutl Religious Thought.* New York: John Wiley & Sons, 1975; Stanley Walens, *Feasting With Cannibals: An Essay on Kwakiutl Cosmology.* Princeton: Princeton University Press, 1981; Helen Codere, ed. *Franz Boas: Kwakiutl Cosmology.* Chicago: University of Chicago Press, 1966; Franz Boas, *Kwakiutl Culture as Reflected in Mythology.* New York: G. E. Stechert, 1935; Franz Boas, "The Social Organization and the Secret Societies of the Kwakiutl Indians," in *Annual Report of the Board of Regents of the Smithsonian Institution, June 30, 1895,* Washington, D.C., 1897; Helen Codere, *Fighting With Property: A Study of Kwakiutl Potlatching and Warfare 1792-1930.* Seattle: University of Washington

Press, 1950; Philip Drucker and Robert F. Heizer, *To Make My Name Good: A Reexamination of the Southern Kwakiutl Potlatch.* Berkeley: University of California Press, 1967.

9. Walens, *Feasting With Cannibals,* pp. 12-15.

10. K. Oberg, "The Kingdom of Ankole in Uganda," in Meyer Fortes and E. E. Evans-Pritchard, eds., *African Political Systems.* London: Oxford University Press, 1940.

11. Melville J. Herskovits, *Dahomey: An Ancient West African Kingdom.* 2 vols. New York: J. J. Augustin, 1938. For the placental origins of *all* poison containers, religious or political, see deMause, *Foundations,* Chapter 7.

12. See Codere, *Fighting With Property.* Surplus-destruction is also one of the functions of the "cargo cults" of newly-contacted primitives.

13. A recent bibliography can be found in Patricia R. Anawalt, "Understanding Aztec Human Sacrifice." *Archaeology* 35(1982): 38-45.

14. Burr C. Brundage, *The Fifth Sun: Aztec Gods, Aztec World.* Austin: University of Texas Press, 1979.

15. Ibid., Chapter 9.

16. Ibid., pp. 205-8.

17. It is significant that this 52-year cycle of the Aztecs, roughly once a lifetime, corresponds very closely to the so-called Kondratieff cycle every 50 years in business activity.

18. The basic analysis is contained in Harvey Brenner, "Estimating the Social Costs of National Economic Policy: Implications for Mental and Physical Health and Clinical Aggression." Joint Economic Committee, U. S. Congress. Washington, D.C.: U. S. Government Printing Office, 1976. I have extended their figures by the increase in unemployment rate for the period 1981-84, estimating the final year at 8 percent average, and adjusting Brenner's figures for total death rates to the overall increase in work force since the 1940-73 base period of their study. Also see references in Sidney Cobb and Stanislaw Kasl, "Termination: The Consequences of Job Loss," Public Health Service, Center for Disease Control, National Institute for Occupational Safety and Health, U.S. Department of Health, Education and Welfare. Washington, D.C., U. S. Government Printing Office, June 1977; Don Stillman, "The Devastating Impact of Plant Relocations," *Working Papers* 5(1978): 49; Stanislaw Kasl, Susan Gore, and Sidney Cobb, "The Experience of Losing a Job: Reported Changes in Health, Symptoms and Illness Behavior," *Psychosomatic Medicine* 37 (1975), pp. 106-22; Barry Bluestone and Bennett Harrison, *The Deindustrialization of America.* New York: Basic Books, 1982, pp. 63-66; and special issue of *American Journal of Orthopsychiatry* (October 1983) on childhood deaths caused by Reaganomics.

19. See Arthur E. Rowse, *One Sweet Guy And What He Is Doing To You.* Washington, D.C.: Consumer News, Inc., 1981; Tracy Freedman and David Weir, "Polluting the Most Vulnerable." *The Nation,* May 14, 1983, pp. 600-603; Barry Bluestone and Bennett Harrison, *Deindustrialization of America,* pp. 63-65; Robert Pear, "Non Profit Groups Are Losing U.S. Aid." *New York Times,* September 2, 1982, p. A18; "Should Congress Reduce Funds for Child Nutrition?" *New York Times,* December 1, 1982, pp. C1 and C19; "Poor Lands, at U.N., Deplore World Economy." *New York Times,* October 14, 1982, p. A6; "Worst Slump in 50 Years Stifles Global Economy." *Washington Post,* January 9, 1983, p. 61; Marshall L. Matz, " 'Bye, School Lunches For the 'Truly Needy.'"*New York Times,* February 23, 1981, p. A30; and Frances Fox Piven and Richard A. Cloward, *The New Class War: Reagan's Attack on the Welfare State and Its Consequences.* New York: Pantheon Books, 1982.

20. Rowse, *One Sweet Guy,* p. 151.

21. *The Washington Post,* June 5, 1983, p. A16.

22. For a description of the theory of psychoclass evolution, see deMause, *Foundations,* Chapter 4 and Glenn Davis, *Childhood and History in America.* New York: Psychohistory Press, 1976.

23. It is astonishing how simple it was for Germany to turn off the 2,000 printing presses in September, 1923, when Schacht stabilized the Mark in one week. See Adam Fergusson, *When Money Dies: The Nightmare of Weimar Collapse.* London: William Kimber, 1975, p. 210.

24. Paul Parin, Fritz Morgenthaler, Goldy Parin-Matthey, *Fear Thy Neighbor as Thyself; Psychoanalysis and Society Among the Anyi of West Africa.* Chicago: University of Chicago Press, 1980, p. 29.

25. William Greider, "The Education of David Stockman," *The Atlantic Monthly,* December, 1981, p. 51.

26. As *Business Week* pointed out, "the nation's biggest corporations are sitting atop a record $80 billion pile of ready cash that could finance a grand boom in capital spending . . . tax measures aimed at generating [even] more cash as a way to stimulate investment probably would not do the trick." "Money is There for the Capital Spending," *Business Week,* September 18, 1978, pp. 97-126. For the argument that "the problem was *not* with the supply of capital funds, but rather the old Keynesian issue of inadequate demand," see Bluestone and Harrison, *The Deindustrialization of America,* p. 198. The Federal Reserve Study which reached identical conclusions is studied in H. Brand, "A Growing Burden on the Workers." *Dissent,* Spring, 1983, p. 138.

27. Senator Baker's comments were made on *Meet The Press,* WCBS-TV, August 2, 1981.

28. On doctors attributing illness to overindulgence in food and sex, see K. Codell Carter, "On the Decline of Bloodletting in Nineteenth Century Medicine." *Journal of Psychoanalytic Anthropology* 5(1982): 219-34.

29. James Tobin, "The Reagan Economic Plan: Supply-Side, Budget and Inflation," in Richard H. Fink, ed., *Supply-Side Economics: A Critical Appraisal.* Frederick, Md.: University Publications of America, 1982, p. 337. Also see John Kenneth Galbraith, "Recession Economics." *New York Review of Books,* February 4, 1982, p. 34.

30. Greider, "The Education of David Stockman," p. 32.

31. Ibid, p. 32.

32. Alexander Cockburn and James Ridgeway, "The Economics of War and Peace (Interview with Seymour Melman.)" *Village Voice,* April 26, 1983. Also see literature cited in James Fallows, "The Great Defense Deception." *New York Review of Books,* May 28, 1981, pp. 15-19.

33. The history of polls on military spending is reviewed in Ben Wattenberg, "Most of the People Still Want More Defense." *The Washington Post,* December 12, 1982, p. C8.

34. George Gilder, *Wealth and Poverty.* New York: Basic Books, 1981, p. 114.

35. Clelia D. Mosher, *The Mosher Survey: Sexual Attitudes of 45 Victorian Women.* Edited by James Hood and Kristine Wenburg. New York: Arno Press, 1980.

36. This *U.S. News* cover illustrates a common symbolic technique of opposing two feelings graphically, so that it is read by the unconscious as saying that "The Reagan Revolution" with its "tax and budget cuts" is *opposed to* (above, superior to) "Our Endless Pursuit of Happiness."

37. Interview with George Gilder in *The Soho News,* December 22, 1981, p. 16. See also Zillah R. Eisenstein, "The Sexual Politics of the New Right: Understanding the 'Crisis of Liberalism' for the 1980s." *Signs: Journal of Women in Culture and Society* 7(1982): 567-88.

38. *The Village Voice,* November 18-24, 1981, p. 21.

39. *New York Times Magazine,* January 18, 1981.

40. *New York Times,* November 20, 1980, p. A34.

41. TRB, *The New Republic,* February 14, 1981, p. 2.

42. Independent News TV, January 30, 1981, 10:30 P.M.

43. James P. Gannon, *Des Moines Sunday Register,* February 22, 1981, p. 7A.

44. Maxwell Newton, *New York Post,* July 28, 1982, p. 49.

45. Cited in Lou Cannon, *Reagan,* p. 406.

46. *Washington Post,* January 2, 1983, p. F1.
47. Gregg Easterbrook, "The Myth of Oppressive Corporate Taxes," *The Atlantic Monthly,* June 1982, p. 59.
48. *New York Times,* Juine 7, 1981, p. 22.
49. *U.S. News & World Report,* July 20, 1981, p. 34.
50. *Washington Post,* July 27, 1981, p. 34.
51. *New York Times,* June 28, 1981, p. 1E.
52. *Time,* July 6, 1981, p. 6.
53. The castration imagery was first analyzed by Rogin, "Ronald Reagan's American Gothic," p. 58.
54. Laurence Barrett, *Gambling With History: Reagan in the White House.* Garden City, New York: Doubleday & Co., 1983, p. 275.

5. CARRYING OUT THE SACRIFICE
"Laser Eyes"

1. *U.S. News & World Report*, September 28, 1981, pp. 64-5.
2. Jo Ann S. Putnam-Scholes, "An Epidemic of Publicity." *Atlantic,* July, 1983, pp. 18-19.
3. *Daily News,* March 14, 1982, p. C2.
4. Frederick Thayer, "Strike Means Friendly Skies For Airlines." *Harper's,* December, 1981, p. 19.
5. Barrett, *Gambling With History,* p. 204.
6. *New York Times*, August 9, 1981, p. 1E.
7. For the insight that Qaddafi was Reagan's "out of control" double, I am indebted to Casper Schmidt, as is the case with so many of the interpretations throughout this book.
8. Haig admitted the "cancer" quote on ABC's "Issues and Answers" program, August 23, 1981.
9. The best reconstruction of the incident can be found in Barrett, *Gambling With History,* pp. 211-13.
10. *Chicago Tribune,* August 23, 1981, p. 1.
11. Ibid., p. 212.
12. Ibid., p. 95.
13. *Time,* August 31, 1981, p. 10.
14. *Daily News*, August 21, 1981, p. 1.
15. *New York Post,* August 24, 1981, p. 7.
16. *Time*, August 31, 1981, p. 12.
17. *Los Angeles Times*, August 23, 1981, Part VI, p. 1.
18. *New York Times*, October 10, 1981, p. 1.
19. In fact, because the Fed's high interest rates caused funds to flow into the U.S. and over-strengthen the dollar, foreign trade dropped even more than total auto sales and housing in 1981; see C. Fred

Bergsten, "The Main Cause of the Recession," *New York Times*, December 21, 1981, p. A27.

20. *Newsweek*, December 21, 1981, p. 63.
21. *Washington Post*, December 13, 1981, p. 30.
22. The best account of the rumor is in *The Soho News*, December 15, 1981, p. 13.
23. Jack Anderson, *New York Post,* June 7, 1982, p. 33; *San Francisco Chronicle*, January 4, 1982, p. 1.
24. *Fridays*, ABC-TV, December 18, 1981.
25. *Today*, NBC-TV, December 18, 1981.
26. Although the U.S. Department of State claimed that "1980 was a record year for international terrorism" (Richard T. Kennedy, Senate Foreign Relations Committee Testimony, June 10, 1981), they admitted that they had only kept statistics for a decade, that their figures were increasingly accurate as time went on and that only 10 Americans were killed in 1980 all over the world, a tragic waste of life, but hardly the "wave of terrorism" which Reagan called "our number one problem."
27. See Lloyd deMause, editor, *The History of Childhood.* New York: Psychohistory Press, 1974, and Davis, *Childhood and History in America.*
28. For a full analysis of the Wolf Man case, from his treatment by Freud to his later treatment by Ruth Mack Brunswick, see M. Gardiner, ed., *The Wolf Man by the Wolf Man.* New York: Basic Books, 1971. My interpretation disagrees with Freud's, which sees the staring wolf eyes as projections of the patient's own staring eyes during the primal scene. Historically, the staring eyes so often betray maternal qualities that they cannot be oedipal projections alone, and must be pre-oedipal.
29. For the Eye of Horus, see Henri Frankfort, *Kingship and the Gods: A Study of Ancient Near Eastern Religion as the Integration of Society & Nature.* Chicago: University of Chicago Press, 1978, pp. 107-9, 127.
30. *Washington Post,* July 8, 1981, p. A1.
31. Jack Anderson, "Strangling the Child-Abuse Program." *Washington Post,* April 4, 1982, p. C7.
32. See, as examples, Kenneth A. Noble, "Are Program Cuts Linked to Increased Infant Deaths?" *New York Times*, February 13, 1983, p. 6E; Barrett, *Gambling With History,* pp. 404-5; Lester C. Thurow, "A Rising Tide of Poverty," *Newsweek,* July 11, 1983, p. 62; Robert Pear, "Job Cuts Cause Loss of Health Coverage For Over 16 Million," *New York Times,* October 31, 1982, p. 1; *Newsweek*, April 5, 1982, pp. 17-27; Arthur E. Rowse, *One Sweet Guy And What He Is Doing To You.* Washington, D.C.: Consumer News, 1981.

33. WPBS-TV, September 12, 1981.

34. Barrett, *Gambling With History*, p. 361.

35. Harrison J. Goldin, "Relieve Hunger with 1 Cent." *New York Times*, November 26, 1982, p. A27. For figures on the cheese distribution, see *New York Times,* January 7, 1982, p. C9, and *New York Times*, July 19, 1983, p. B7.

36. See footnote 28 of Chapter 1 of this book.

37. Reagan address to International Association of Chiefs of Police, September 28, 1981.

38. *New York Post,* October 5, 1981, p. 3.

39. *Washington Post,* September 26, 1981, p. A23.

40. Ibid.

41. *Los Angeles Times,* December 5, 1982, Part IV, p. 5.

42. *Los Angeles Times*, March 21, 1982, p. 1.

43. *The Washington Spectator*, November 1, 1981, p. 2.

44. *The Washington Monthly,* July, August, 1982, pp. 7 and 37.

45. *Newsweek*, March 8, 1982, p. 77; *U.S. News & World Report*, September 21, 1981, cover.

46. Greider, "Education of David Stockman," p. 51.

47. Lewis Lapham, *Washington Post*, September 26, 1981, p. A23.

48. *New York Times*, September 20, 1981, p. E1.

49. *New York*, November 2, 1981, p. A3.

50. *Washington Post*, November 22, 1981, p. A3.

51. *New York*, November 2, 1981, p. 19.

52. *New York Times,* February 15, 1982, p. A12.

53. *Washington Post*, January 24, 1982, p. 1.

54. *Washington Post*, April 4, 1982, p. A3.

55. *New York Times,* February 8, 1982, p. A19.

56. *Washington Post*, November 8, 1981, p. A2.

57. *Washington Post*, September 27, 1981, p. A3.

58. WNBC-TV, Six O'Clock News, March 23, 1982.

59. WNET-TV, The MacNeil-Lehrer Report, December 17, 1981.

60. *New York Times,* December 11, 1981, p. A22.

61. *Newsweek*, November 16, 1981, p. 88.

62. *Mother Jones*, August 1983, p. 52.

63. *Miami Herald*, March 21, 1982, p. F1.

64. WNET-TV, October 7, 1981.

65. *New York Times,* January 2, 1983, p. 14E.

66. WNBC-TV, Six O'Clock News, November 12, 1981.

67. *Newsweek*, April 12, 1982, p. 18.

68. *Washington Post*, March 21, 1982, p. D5.

69. *New York Times*, May 27, 1982, p. B22.

70. *Washington Post*, May 2, 1982, p. A2.

71. Evidence that actual memories of birth are remembered and replayed during group-fantasies is presented in deMause, *Foundations*, Chapter 7, "The Fetal Origins of History."
72. *New York Post,* March 2, 1982, p. 15.
73. *New York Times*, March 16, 1982, p. A22.
74. *New York Post*, April 16, 1982, p. 70.
75. Ibid.

6. TRIAL WARS
"What a Cute Little War."

1. *Washington Post*, April 25, 1982, p. A21.
2. Max Hastings and Simon Jenkins, *The Battle for the Falklands*. New York: W. W. Norton & Co., 1983, p. 325.
3. All the British "mistakes"—actually hidden messages—are detailed in ibid., pp. 1-60 and in the *Sunday Times* of London Insight Team, *War in the Falklands: The Full Story*. New York: Harper & Row, 1982.
4. Hastings and Jenkins, *Battle for the Falklands*, p. 65.
5. *The Nation*, March 6, 1982, p. 261; the Cuban blockade scheme is mentioned by Jorge Luis Borges in Tad Szulc, "A Voice of Peace, Alone." *Parade*, November 14, 1982, p. 5. The blockade was first suggested by Reagan in his election campaign; see Ronnie Dugger, *On Reagan*. New York: McGraw-Hill Book Co., 1983, p. 360.
6. Hastings and Jenkins, *Battle for the Falklands*, pp. 103 and 173.
7. For evidence of Galtieri's conviction that the U.S. would back him on the invasion, see the *New York Times*, May 2, 1982, p. 2E, *The New Republic*, June 9, 1982, p. 12 and *Newsweek*, May 17, 1982, p. 30.
8. For the process of delegation of hidden family wishes, see Helm Stierlin, *Separating Parents and Adolescents*. New York, 1974.
9. Hastings and Jenkins, *Battle for the Falklands,* p. 108.
10. *Inquiry*, May 17, 1982, p. 8.
11. *New York Post*, April 6, 1982, p. 35.
12. *Newsweek*, April 26, 1982, p. 92.
13. "Nightline," WABC-TV, May 20, 1982.
14. *Washington Post*, May 30, 1982, p. C8.
15. *Time,* January 24, 1964, p. 54.
16. Doris Kearns, *Lyndon Johnson and the American Dream*. New York: Harper & Row, 1976, p. 251. Also see Chapter 3, "War" in Susan Brownmiller, *Against Our Will: Men, Women and Rape*. New York: Simon & Schuster, 1975.

17. For details on Vietnam group-fantasies, see David Beisel, "The Psychohistorical Origins of the Vietnam War," *Journal of Psychohistory* 11 (1984): in press.
18. "Vietnam: A Television History. Part 5." WPBS-TV, October 25, 1983.
19. Ibid., Part 4, October 18, 1983.
20. *New York Post*, May 14, 1982, p. 5.
21. *New York Times*, April 7, 1982, p. A23.
22. Hastings and Jenkins, *Battle for the Falklands*, p. 340.
23. Here, again, the cover artist puts the headline "Mideast Nightmare: Search for a Way Out?" over "End of the Permissive Society," a layout which represents to the unconscious that the "nightmare" of war in the mideast is a "way out" from "the permissive society."
24. The language is that of Reagan's friendly biographer, Laurence Barrett, *Gambling With History,* p. 271.
25. The admission by Sharon of Reagan's secret agreement was revealed on "Nightline," WABC-TV, June 24, 1981.
26. Personal communication, Paul Smirnoff, Executive Producer, Metromedia News. President Carter also said Israel had received approval from Washington for the invasion; see Dugger, *On Reagan*, p. 388.
27. Barrett, *Gambling With History*, p. 280.
28. *Los Angeles Times,* June 9, 1982, p. 7.
29. Rowland Evans and Robert Novak, *New York Post,* July 7, 1982, p. 31.
30. *Washington Post,* July 4, 1982, p. B1.
31. *Village Voice*, August 10, 1982, p. 8.
32. *Philadelphia Inquirer*, July 3, 1981, p. 1.
33. *New York Post*, June 15, 1981, p. 27.
34. John Frosch, *The Psychotic Process*. New York: International Universities Press, 1983, pp. 63-64.
35. Dugger, *On Reagan*, p. 405.
36. Ibid., p. 404.
37. *New York Times*, May 30, 1982.
38. *New York Post* October 21, 1981, p. 12.
39. *New Yorker*, July 19, 1982, p. 24.
40. See William Martin, "Waiting For The End," *The Atlantic Monthly,* June 1982, pp. 31-37.
41. *Esquire*, November 1982, p. 16.
42. *New York Times*, November 12, 1981, p. 24.
43. Dugger, *On Reagan*, p. 394.
44. For references to all three levels of Aztec sacrifice, see Brundage, *The Fifth Sun.*

45. *New York Times*, September 30, 1982, p. 1.
46. *Washington Post,* October 25, 1983, p. A6.
47. *Daily News*, October 25, 1983, p. 5.
48. *Daily News*, November 5, 1982, p. 2.
49. *New York Times*, November 5, 1983, p. 7.
50. Casper Schmidt, "The Use of the Gallup Poll as a Psychohistorical Tool," *Journal of Psychohistory* 10 (1982):141-162; Casper Schmidt, "A Differential Poison Index from the Gallup Poll," *Journal of Psychohistory* 10(1983): 523-532; Casper Schmidt and Lloyd deMause, "An Update on Reagan's America: Group-Fantasies on the Way to Collapse." Fifth Annual Convention, International Psychohistorical Association, Hunter College, June 12, 1982; radio broadcasts on National Public Radio Network and WBAI.
51. Lt. Col. John H. Buchanan, "Honduras/Nicaragua—War Without Winners," testimony of September 21, 1982, reprinted in *NACLA Report on the Americas*, September/October 1982, pp. 2-10.
52. Cited in *The New Republic*, October 24, 1983, p. 7.
53. Boyarsky, *Ronald Reagan,* pp. 35-38.
54. T. D. Allman, "Reagan's Manifest Destiny." *Harper's*, September 1983, pp. 30-39; Walter LeFeber, *Inevitable Revolutions: The United States in Central America.* New York: W. W. Norton Co., 1983.
55. As the *Washington Post* put it, "Some diplomats in the area are disturbed about the way in which the Vietnam hands suddenly latched onto Central America, as if it were a solid rung on their career ladder after years of drifting in the wake of Vietnam." (November 28, 1982, p. C3)
56. *Time*, October 17, 1983, p. 49.
57. Case history described to author by Casper Schmidt, M.D.
58. *Washington Post*, May 9, 1982, p. A21.
59. *Newsweek*, November 7, 1983, p. 137; Janet Raloff, "Beyond Armageddon," *Science News*, November 12, 1983, pp. 314-17.
60. Stuart D. Asch, "Suicide, and the Hidden Executioner." *International Review of Psycho-Analysis* 7(1980): 51-60.
61. Dugger, *On Reagan*, p. 401; Robert Scheer, *With Enough Shovels: Reagan, Bush & Nuclear War.* New York: Random House, 1983; Fred Kaplan, *The Wizards of Armageddon.* New York: Simon & Schuster, 1983.
62. Dugger, *On Reagan,* p. 400.
63. Gallup poll, cited in *Newsweek*, October 5, 1981, p. 35.
64. Patrick O'Heffernan, Amory B. Lovins and L. Hunter Lovins, *The First Nuclear World War.* New York: William Morrow & Co., 1983, pp. 158-9.

65. Ibid., pp. 16, 163-4.
66. Ibid., p. 156.
67. Ibid., p. 241.
68. Ibid., pp. 15-57.
69. Ibid., p. 418; the statement was by Rep. Downey, about the 10-minute delivery time of Trident 2, and is even more applicable to the 6-minute delivery time of Pershing 2.
70. *Chicago Tribune*, January 9, 1983, p. 1.

7. THE POISON BUILDS UP
"There's a Virus in Our Bloodstream"

1. Cited in *The New Leader*, October 5, 1982, p. 7.
2. Robert Furlow, "Treasury Maps Out Record Borrowing," *New York Post*, July 29, 1982, p. 42; "Bankruptcies Still Soar," *Richmond Times-Dispatch*, September 2, 1982, p. E1; Peter Kilborn, "Study Finds Low '82 Level for Unemployment Claims," *New York Times*, September 9, 1983, p. D17; Marion Wright Edelman, "Death By Poverty, Arms, Or Moral Numbness" *American Journal of Orthopsychiatry* 53 (1983): 593-601; Robert Reno, "Children Carry Poverty Burden," *Newsday*, August 7, 1983, p. 78; Peter Kilborn, "Americans Saving Less Now Than Before the '81 Tax Act," *New York Times*, September 6, 1983, p. 1; Jack Egan, "Banks on the Brink," *New York*, October 25, 1982, p. 28.
3. WNBC-TV, "Nightly News," November 3, 1982.
4. *Time*, December 13, 1982, p. 12.
5. Metromedia News, July 11, 1982.
6. WABC-TV, December 24, 1982.
7. Maxwell Newton, *New York Post,* January 4, 1983, p. 39.
8. Steven R. Weisman, "Reaganomics and the President's Men," *New York Times Magazine,* October 24, 1982, pp. 26-27.
9. *Newsweek,* December 13, 1982, p. 70. For evidence that we were repeating actual memories of the failing placenta, our first "heart," see deMause, Chapter 7, "Fetal Origins of History," *Foundations*.
10. *Atlantic Monthly*, April, 1983, p. 10.
11. David Beisel, *Dance of Death. An Inquiry Into the Origins of the Second World War.* Forthcoming.
12. *New York Times*, June 6, 1982, p. 20E.
13. *New York Post*, April 28, 1982, p. 39.
14. Reagan said this on January 25, 1983, in reference to drug pushers.
15. See *New York Times*, November 30, 1982, p. 1; *The Nation*, June 18, 1983, pp. 754-5; *New York Times*, November 28, 1983, p. 23.
16. *Daily News*, September 10, 1982, p. 39.

17. For details, see Cannon, *Reagan*, p. 288 and Rowse, *One Sweet Guy*, p. 84.
18. Tony Thomas, *The Films of Ronald Reagan*. Secaucus, N.J.: Citadel Press, 1981, p. 61.
19. Speech by Roosevelt rebroadcast on WNET-TV, August 9, 1983. This paranoid fear of infection from refugees was the real reason why America kept Jews out for so long and didn't save more of them.
20. *U.S. News*, September 16, 1963, pp. 98-101.
21. *Time*, August 2, 1982, cover.
22. *Reader's Digest*, February, 1983, cover.
23. *Mother Jones*, November 1982, p. 36.
24. Reagan's phallic charts showing American impotence are reproduced in *The New York Times*, November 23, 1982, p. A12.
25. See Casper Schmidt, "The Fantasy Structure of AIDS, and Other Forms of Epidemic Hysteria." *Journal of Psychohistory* 11(1984): forthcoming.
26. See Tim Reiterman, *Raven: The Untold Story of The Rev. Jim Jones and His People*. New York: E. P. Dutton, 1983. The Jonestown parallel was pointed out to me by Casper Schmidt.
27. *The Des Moines Sunday Register*, October 17, 1982, p. 1.
28. *Time*, February 23, 1981, p. 12.
29. *New York Post*, October 1, 1982, p. 1.
30. *National Enquirer,* October 6, 1982, p. 2; *New York Post*, October 1, 1982, p. 1.
31. *New York Post*, December 15, 1982, p. 2.
32. *New York Post*, October 22, 1982, p. 4; ibid., October 26, 1982, p. 2; ibid., January 25, 1983, p. 5; *Time*, November 8, 1982, p. 27.
33. *New York Post*, October 29, 1982, p. 1.
34. *Time*, November 8, 1982, p. 27; *Washington Post*, October 31, 1982, p. A22.
35. *New York Times*, November 3, 1982, p. A27.
36. *Village Voice*, March 22, 1983, p. 18.
37. *New York*, February 7, 1983, p. 42.
38. *New York Times*, October 20, 1983, p. B7.
39. *Chicago Tribune*, June 6, 1982, p. 1, Section 2.
40. *Kansas City Star*, January 20, 1983, p. 1.
41. *USA Today*, June 23, 1983, p. 1; *New York Times*, June 25, 1983, p. 1.
42. The first sentence for chemical castration was given in February, 1982; for a summary of the sentences, see *Washington Post,* December 24, 1983, p. A7.
43. *National Review*, November 11, 1983, p. 1411.
44. *New York,* June 20, 1983, p. 27.

45. See Chapter 7, deMause, *Foundations*. For strikingly similar group-fantasies among the *Freikorps*, see Klaus Theweleit, *Maennerphantasien*. Frankfurt: Roter Stern Verlag, 1977.

46. *New York*, June 20, 1983, p. 28; *Washington Post*, July 11, 1983, p. 1.

47. *New York Times*, August 7, 1983, p. E21.

48. *New York Times*, December 5, 1983, p. B6.

49. *New York Times*, October 3, 1983, p. 1.

50. *Newsweek,* August 8, 1983, p. 30.

51. Cited in *The Washington Post*, January 30, 1983, p. A3.

52. *Washington Post*, January 16, 1983, p. A3.

53. William Schneider, *Los Angeles Times*, January 2, 1983, p. 1, Part IV.

54. *Washington Post*, January 30, 1983, p. A3.

55. *Washington Post*, May 10, 1982, p. A15.

56. *New York Times,* March 9, 1983, p. A18.

57. Cited in the *Los Angeles Times*, November 20, 1983, Part IV, p. 1.

58. The citation is from Bowman's appearance on "The MacNeill-Lehrer News Hour," WNET-TV, November 10, 1983. Also see his statements in "Star Wars—Pie in the Sky," *New York Times,* December 14, 1983, p. A35.

59. *Washington Post*, March 26, 1983, p. 1.

60. John Tirman, "Star Wars—From Scenario to Fact," *The Nation*, December 24, 1983, p. 664.

61. William E. Burrows, "Skywalking With Reagan," *Harper's*, January 1984, p. 56.

62. Reagan made this statement about Social Security to open his March 25, 1983 news conference, but the emotional content referred more to his dramatic Star Wars speech of two days earlier.

64. Jack Anderson, *New York Post*, December 26, 1983, p. 21.

65. *Washington Post*, June 21, 1983, p. A7.

66. "Washington Week in Review," WNET-TV, October 7, 1983. The "poison spider" image is cited in Howard Stein, "The Scope of Psycho-Geography." *Journal of Psychoanalytic Anthropology* 7(1984): in press. On the immigration imagery, see James Fallows, "Immigration: How It's Affecting Us," *The Atlantic Monthly*, November 1983, pp. 45-48.

8. THE POISON IS DUMPED ABROAD
"There's a Fire in Our Front Yard."

1. For Reagan's sudden shift upward in the polls after his March war speeches, see *Time*, July 18, 1983, pp. 9-11.

2. *Time*, July 18, 1983, p. 14.

3. *Newsweek*, March 14, 1983, p. 16.
4 *Time*, March 21, 1983, p. 12.
5. *U.S. News*, October 3, 1983, p. 22.
6. *Time*, June 28, 1983, p. 32.
7. *New Republic*, April 18, 1983, p. 9.
8. *Newsweek*, March 21, 1983, p. 18.
9. Reagan used these action words in his April 19 statement on the President's Commission on Strategic Forces.
10. *New Republic*, April 4, 1983, p. 7.
11. Ibid.
12. *New York Times,* March 30, 1983, p. A31.
13. *Daily News*, July 4, 1983, p. 2.
14. *Washington Post*, July 24, 1983, p. C1; May 26, 1983, p. A3.
15. The full story of the B1 approval can be found in the *Dallas Times Herald*, February 12, 1984, pp. 1 and 6.
16. David Morrison, "Conventional Madness: The Next European War." *Inquiry*, February 1984, pp. 21-24.
17. *New York Times*, March 6, 1983, p. 1E.
18. "Face the Nation," WCBS-TV, May 23, 1983.
19. *New York Times*, March 6, 1983, p. 1E.
20. A summary of the buildup of these bases is in *The Washington Post*, February 17, 1984, p. A25.
21. *New York Times*, November 8, 1983, p. A12.
22. *Washington Post*, August 21, 1983, p. C1.
23. *New York Times*, July 1, 1983, p. 1.
24. For one priest's eyewitness account of *contra* terrorist raids and shooting of innocent women and children, see *In These Times*, February 8-14, 1984, p. 16. For the CIA's *contra* pay scale, see *Minneapolis Tribune*, November 27, 1983, p. 1.
25. *Los Angeles Times*, April 3, 1983, p. 1.
26. *New York Post*, May 23, 1983, p. 33.
27. *New York Times*, July 31, 1983, p. 1.
28. *Washington Post*, July 27, 1983, p. 1.
29. *Newsweek*, June 6, 1983, cover.
30. For how Honduran Gen. Martinez used the deaths of the two journalists to claim "the Sandanistas are attacking us," see *USA Today*, p. 7A. Few newspapers printed the later information that it was a mine—and not Nicaraguan artillery—that killed the journalists.
31. WCBS-TV, "Nightly News," July 23, 1983; *New York Post*, July 25, 1983, p. 2.
32. *New York Times,* July 17, 1983, p. 1.
33. *Newsday*, August 14, 1983, p. 15.
34. Ibid.

35. *Washington Post*, July 31, 1983, p. A3.
36. *Time*, August 1, 1983, p. 10.
37. *New York Times*, July 23, 1983, p. 1.
38. *New York Post*, July 20, 1983, p. 1.
39. *Washington Post*, July 25, 1983, p. 1.
40. WABC-TV, "This Week With David Brinkley," July 24, 1983.
41. *New York Times*, July 28, 1983, p. A11.
42. *New York Times*, July 22, 1983, p. A23.
43. *New York Times,* August 9, 1983, p. A23.
44. *Newsday*, August 7, 1983, p. 6.
45. *New York Times*, July 24, 1983, p. D1.
46. Ibid.
47. *Washington Post*, July 31, 1983, p. D8.
48. *Washington Post,* July 26, 1983, p. A10.
49. *New York Times*, July 26, p. A20.
50. *Washington Post*, August 2, 1983, p. A3.
51. Ibid.
52. *New York Post*, September 20, 1983, p. 31.
53. *U.S. News*, July 25, 1983, cover.
54. *Newsweek*, September 12, 1983, p. 44.
55. *Time*, September 12, 1983, p. 14; *Orlando Sentinel*, September 11, 1983, p. G1; *Chicago Tribune*, September 11, 1983, Sec. 4, p. 1.
56. James Bamford, "The Last Flight of KAL 007." *Washington Post Magazine*, January 8, 1984, p. 5.
57. Cited in *The Washington Spectator*, November 1, 1983, p. 2.
58. Cited in the *Village Voice*, September 27, 1983, p. 14 and *The Washington Spectator*, November 1, 1983, p. 3.
59. Bamford, "Last Flight," p. 4; *Miami Herald*, September 11, 1983, p. 1; R. W. Johnson, "KAL 007: Unanswered Questions." *World Press Review*, March 1984, pp. 23-26.
60. Ibid., pp. 4-8; David Baker, *The Shape of Wars to Come.* New York: Stein and Day, 1981, p. 230.
61. *Washington Post*, December 31, 1983, p. A6; also see *People*, December 26, 1983, p. 41 on the Melvin Belli Lawsuit.
62. Information on these points can be found in Bamford, "Last Flight," pp. 4-8 and *Washington Post*, December 31, 1983, p. A6.
63. *New York Times,* October 7, 1983, p. 1.
64. Bamford, "Last Flight," p. 6.
65. *Village Voice*, September 27, 1983, p. 14.
66. *Daily News*, September 19, 1983, p. 30.
67. WNBC-TV, "Eleven O'Clock News," September 1, 1983.
68. *Orlando Sentinal*, September 11, 1983, p. G1.
69. *New York Post*, September 3, 1983, p. 1.
70. *Chicago Tribune*, October 2, 1983, Sec. 4, p. 1.

71. *New York Times*, September 2, 1983, p. A23.
72. A roundup of editorial reaction to KAL 007 can be found in William Boot, "Capital Letter," *Columbia Journalism Review*, November/December 1983, pp. 27-30.
73. *New York Times*, September 25, 1983, p. 1E.
74. *Chicago Tribune*, September 4, 1983, Sec. 1, p. 12.
75. *New York Times,* September 3, 1983, p. 7.
76. *Newsweek*, September 19, 1983, p. 38.
77. WABC-TV, September 4, 1983.
78. WNBC-TV, September 4, 1983.
79. Metromedia News, September 8, 1983.
80. *New York Post*, September 13, 1983, p. 29.
81. *Washington Post*, September 18, 1983. p. C7.
82. Metromedia News, September 8, 1983.
83. *New York Post*, September 26, 1983, p. 31.

9. KILLING THE POISONED
"The Wrath of Ron"

1. *Inquiry*, July 1983, p. 17.
2. Sara Davidson, *Friends of the Opposite Sex*. Garden City, N.Y.: Doubleday & Co., 1984, p. 61.
3. *New York Post*, September 13, 1983, p. 1.
4. *The New Republic*, October 10, 1983, p. 11.
5. *Miami Herald*, October 2, 1983, p. 1D.
6. *Washington Post*, October 2, 1983, p. A3.
7. *New York Times*, October 2, 1983, p. E4.
8. *Report of the DOD Commission on Beirut International Airport Terrorist Act, October 23, 1983*. Department of Defense, 20 December 1983, pp. 49-50.
9. Ibid., pp. 51 and 89.
10. *New York Post*, October 24, 1983, p. 7; *New York Times*, October 25, 1983, p. 1 and November 2, 1983, p. 1.
11. *New York Post*, February 20, 1984, p. 5.
12. For a thorough analysis of Reagan's apocalyptic beliefs, see Ronnie Dugger, "Does Reagan Expect a Nuclear Armageddon?" *Washington Post*, April 8, 1984, p. C1.
13. *Time*, January 2, 1984, p. 56.
14. *New York Times,* October 25, 1983, p. A15.
15. *New York Times*, October 25, 1983, p. A10.
16. The quote on the killing of the son is from clips shown on "Night Line," WABC-TV, March 22, 1984; a full analysis of the "grief reporting" of Beirut can be found in C. Fraser Smith, "Reporting

Grief: Marine Families Review the Press Invasion," *Washington Journalism Review*, March 1984, pp. 21-22, 58.

17. *New York Times*, October 26, 1983, p. A7.
18. Norman Kirkham, "Landing plan 6 months old," *Sunday Telegraph* [London], October 30, 1983, p. 40.
19. *The Economist*, March 10, 1984, p. 31; also see *Washington Post*, October 28, 1983, p. 13.
20. *The Atlanta Journal and Constitution*, November 6, 1983, p. 1.
21. Eyewitness accounts of the island the week of the invasion can be found in "Grenada: Diary of an invasion." *Race & Class* 23 (1984): 15-26. Although the Department of Defense official report, "Grenada: A Preliminary Report," Washington, D. C., December 16, 1983, said "riots and looting were reported," no source is given for this statement (p. 36).
22. *Los Angeles Times*, November 6, 1983, Part IV, p. 3.
23. *Washington Post*, October 26, 1983, p. A11; *New York Times*, November 1, 1983, p. A16.
24. *Los Angeles Times,* November 6, 1983, Part IV, p. 3.
25. *New York Times*, October 25, 1983, p. A5.
26. Ibid.
27. *New York Times*, October 29, 1983, p. 7.
28. *Washington Post*, October 27, 1983, p. A8.
29. *Washington Post*, November 15, 1983, p. A15.
30. William Steif, "Reagan's Island," *The Progressive*, January 1984, p. 19.
31. U.S. Department of State, Bureau of Public Affairs, "The Larger Importance of Greneda," November 4, 1983, p. 4.
32. Dozens of similar U.S. "misinformations" are cited in *New York Times*, November 6, 1983, p. 20.
33. *Village Voice,* November 22, 1983, p. 12.
34. *Village Voice*, November 8, 1983, p. 8.
35. "Grenada: diary," p. 20.
36. *Washington Post*, November 6, 1983, p. 1.
37. "Nightline," WABC-TV, October 27, 1983.
38. An analysis of videotapes I made of the TV coverage revealed that whenever the students were pressed by the reporter as to whether they were in fact in danger before the invasion or because of it, they admitted it was only American firepower they were speaking about. Virtually no one watching the students, however, could internalize this fact, and all commentators went on describing "the danger the students were in" which the invasion "saved them from."
39. *Washington Post*, October 28, 1983, p. 1; *New York Times*, October 27, 1983, p. 1.

40. *New York Times*, October 28, 1983, p. 5; *Washington Post*, November 13, 1983, p. B5.
41. *New York Times*, October 28, 1983, p. 17.
42. *New York Times*, November 6, 1983, p. 20.
43. *Daily News*, November 11, 1983, p. 6.
44. *The Economist*, March 10, 1984, p. 32.
45. *The Observer*, October 30, 1983, p. 9.
46. The official Pentagon body count of 18 Americans, 47 Cubans and 21 Grenadans undercounted the number of Grenadans killed; see footnote 74 to this chapter.
47. It is possible that Reagan, like his friend Rev. Jerry Fallwell, who is also a religious fundamentalist, felt the Marines were "raptured in a twinkling of an eye" into heaven; see Ronnie Dugger, "Does Reagan Expect an Armageddon?" p. C4.
48. *New York Times*, October 26, 1983, p. A22; *Washington Post*, November 3, 1983, p. A3.
49. *The Observer*, October 30, 1983, p. 11.
50. George Will, *Newsweek*, November 7, 1983, p. 142.
51. Patrick Buchanan, *New York Post*, October 27, 1983, p. 27.
52. *Washington Post*, October 30, 1983, p. A18.
53. "Night Line," WABC-TV, October 27, 1983.
54. "Nightly News," WNBC-TV, December 13, 1983; *Daily News*, December 18, 1983, p. 6.
55. John Hess, Metromedia News, November 10, 1983.
56. *Washington Post*, November 24, 1983, p. 1.
57. *New York Times*, November 7, 1983, p. 1.
58. *Dallas Times Herald*, October 30, 1983, p. 17.
59. Gallup news release, March 4, 1984, p. 1.
60. The story was in his December 12, 1984 speech, and was later found not to have occurred.
61. *New York Times*, December 11, 1983, p. 1.
62. *Chicago Tribune*, November 20, 1983, p. 1.
63. *New York Post*, November 9, 1983, p. 36.
64. Cited in *The Nation*, April 7, 1984, p. 404.
65. *New York Times*, March 20, 1984, p. 3.
66. For a psychohistorical analysis of the phenomenon, see David Beisel, "Thoughts on the Cabbage Patch Kids," *Journal of Psychohistory* 11 (1984): in press.
67. Cannibalistic wishes regularly precede wars; for an analysis of the intrapsychic dynamics of cannibalistic fantasies toward children, see Joyce McDougall, "A Child is Being Eaten," *Contemporary Psychoanalysis* 16 (1980): 417-459.

68. Attacks by terrorists in America in 1983 had dropped to 31 from 51 in 1982; see *U.S. News*, January 9, 1984, p. 26.

69. *Newsweek*, December 26, 1983, p. 14.

70. *New York Times*, December 14, 1983, p. A14.

71. *New York Post*, April 16, 1984, p. 29.

72. *New York Post*, November 4, 1983, p. 43.

73. For Reagan's quote and an analysis of his offensive plans, see Tad Szulc, "The Tough New Line on Central America," *Los Angeles Times*, September 18, 1983, Part IV, p. 1.

74. *Daily News*, April 17, 1984, p. 22.

75. "Nightly News," WNBC-TV, February 4, 1984.

INDEX

DATE DUE

OC 21 '03		

DEMCO 38-297